PENGUIN BOOKS

The Ten (Food) Commandments

Jay Rayner is a journalist, writer, broadcaster and musician, with a pronounced love of pig and a fine collection of flowery shirts. He has been the restaurant critic for the *Observer* for over fifteen years, presents the culinary panel show *The Kitchen Cabinet* for BBC Radio 4 and is a regular on both *The One Show* and *Masterchef*. He performs live all over the country, both with his jazz quartet and in one-man shows. A new live show based on *The Ten (Food) Commandments* will be touring Britain throughout 2016 and 2017. He lives in south London with his wife and two sons. This is his ninth book.

The Ten (Food) Commandments

JAY RAYNER

PENGUIN BOOKS

PENGUIN BOOKS

UK | USA | Canada | Ireland | Australia
India | New Zealand | South Africa

Penguin Books is part of the Penguin Random House group of companies
whose addresses can be found at global.penguinrandomhouse.com.

First published 2016
001

Copyright © Jay Rayner Ltd, 2016

The moral right of the author has been asserted

Typeset in Dante MT Std by Palimpsest Book Production Ltd, Falkirk, Stirlingshire

Printed in Great Britain by Clays Ltd, St Ives plc

A CIP catalogue record for this book is available from the British Library

ISBN: 978–0–241–97669–2

www.greenpenguin.co.uk

For my sister, Amanda, who had to budge up
at the table when I arrived.

Contents

Go shout it from the mountain top

The prophet Moses was many things: rebel leader, font of moral-
ity, poster boy for dodgy orienteering. On the tricky matter of
your dinner he was less helpful, at least if the Ten Commandments are anything to go by. If we assume they really were
dictated by God and not something Moses cooked up when he
was alone on the mountain top after having stomped off in a
huff, the first four reveal the Maker to be a touch self-absorbed.
It's all 'You shall have no other gods before me' and 'You shall not
misuse the name of the Lord your God.' Really! Some people!

That's followed by boilerplate stuff prohibiting murder, theft
and lying, before you get to the only one which in any way pertains
to ingredients: the instruction not to covet thy neighbour's oxen.
Always tricky: there are some damn attractive oxen out there.

This is the great failing of the original Ten Commandments.
They really don't offer those of us located in the twenty-first
century much in the way of guidance when it comes to thinking
about our relationship with our food. And Lord knows we need it.

Rabbinical scholars will point out that those original Ten
Commandments were actually only the headlines, rather than
the full text. This is true, in as much as anything in the Bible
is true. According to the great rabbis, Moses was not given just
ten rules on the mountain top. He was given 613, which would
have presented a serious challenge to the masons charged
with carving them into tablets of stone, let alone to Moses,
who would then have had to carry them down off the summit.
No wonder he decided to stick with bullet points and leave the
fine print in his back pocket.

An examination of those 613 as listed by the twelfth-century scholar Maimonides reveals them to be curious and, in places, eccentric. Some of them – the ones about making sure to lend to the poor, or the imperative for judges to be honest – are about the construction of civil society. Others read like building regulations: '494. You must make a guard rail around a flat roof.' That's just basic health and safety. And then there are those that appear to be predicting the rise of www.pornhub.com and are designed to prohibit a few of the more recondite categories: '146. You must not have sexual relations with a woman and her daughter'; '151. You must not have sexual relations with your father's brother's wife.' Thank God my dad was an only child or I might have found the latter seriously challenging.

Elsewhere, however, these 613 do actually include an awful lot on how and what to eat. Numbers 176 to 208 are all about food choices. For example, number 192 is the instruction not to eat blood, the commandment which underlies the koshering of meat, by the removal of all plasma. It is also therefore the commandment which has made centuries of bar mitzvah dinners an ordeal by dry rubber chicken. Many of the rest seem at best odd and at worst proof that the Jewish God was just the pickiest of eaters. Number 185 is an instruction not to eat non-kosher maggots, which presumably means it's okay to eat the kosher ones. Number 194 declares that we must not eat 'the sinew of the thigh'. Really? But that's my favourite bit.

As a diehard atheist, it's all proof to me that He simply doesn't exist. The French philosopher Descartes argued that God is perfect, the concept of perfection including existence, ergo God must exist. For Descartes, philosophy was a fairground ride that just went round and round.

But if He is genuinely perfect He would also have to be the perfect dinner guest, rather than the nightmarish faddy eater the 613 commandments reveal Him to be. God would be all 'No crab for me, please' and 'You know FULL WELL I don't do cheeseburgers.' The God of the commandments, 613 or otherwise, would not be the perfect dinner guest.

Certainly none of this provides the guidance people need when it comes to making modern food choices. Both the headline Ten and the remaining 603 commandments were devised at a time when 'street food' meant discarded offcuts found in the gutter by the destitute; at a time when the word 'dirty' was reserved for things like a chap having sexual relations with a woman and her daughter, rather than for a hamburger with seven too many toppings; when people still bought ingredients rather than 'sourced' them. It was all so much simpler then. After all, the vast majority of decisions around food in Moses' day were to do with basic nourishment, trying not to poison yourself and avoiding upsetting a vengeful god.

In these, the early years of the twenty-first century, how and what we eat is so very much more important than any of that. Forget upsetting a vengeful god. There's worrying about what your friends would think if you tried to eat a hot dog with a knife and fork. There's the complex business of knowing whether the global food multinationals are trying to turn a quick buck by killing you one sugar-infested meal at a time. And there's the dismal, soul-destroying experience of sitting in front of the fridge just before you pack it with the new weekly shop, and wondering whether the amount of things that you didn't eat last week and are now wasted mark you out as an EVIL PERSON. (I'll keep it brief: they do. Sorry.)

What does all this tell us? It tells us that we need a new set of hand-tooled, subject-specific food commandments, custom-engineered for the modern food-obsessed age.

Which in turn means we need our very own culinary Moses; someone with the scholarship, dignity, insight and teeth to stand in judgement on everyone else.

I know just the man.

Oh, come on. Who else could it be?

I have a beard flecked with grey. I have shaggy hair and, though I say it myself, I look super-hot in flowing robes. (They rather flatter the more generous figure.) And yes, I really do have all my own teeth. I wouldn't mind having someone else's teeth, but I'll settle for mine. They've seen me this far.

So come with me as I lay down the law; as I deal once and for all with the question of whether it really is ever okay to covet thy neighbour's oxen (it is), how important it is to eat with your hands (very important indeed), and whether you should cut off the fat (you shouldn't).

I will give you guidance on worshipping leftovers and why you should not mistake food for pharmaceuticals which can cure you of all known diseases, especially cancer. (A quick heads-up: there is not a single foodstuff the eating of which will protect you from cancer. Not even a little bit.) I will insist that thou shalt cook while also not running from the stinkiest of foods, even if they smell of death. The best foods in life smell lightly of death.

I will insist that thou shalt honour thy pig. Or anybody else's pig for that matter. Because everything is improved by the application of a little pig.

In this I recognize that I will be somewhat at odds with Moses and the original commandments he handed down to the children of Israel. But I swear that if he'd ever been introduced to a proper bacon sandwich, one made with soft white bread, and crisped, still-warm streaky and a smear of brown sauce, he would have been with me. The whole prohibition-on-pork thing would never have been in there.

I am a TERRIBLE Jew.

Traditionally, the creation of moral codes like this has been thought experiments, philosophical exercises conducted more in the head than in the world. And there will be a bit of that. I have long been a fan of sitting down. It's part of my skill set. But to get to grips with the intricacies of these new commandments requires a more expansive approach. That's one of the great things about food. The act of eating well, of understanding our food and the part it plays in our lives, demands an inquisitive mind. All ingredients have stories of their own, and I intend to tell them. So come with me as I frame a set of commandments based not just on lofty ideas, but on clear-eyed experience, a bit of reading, and talking to the right people, which is to say, the ones who agree with me. And appetite. I have appetites like south London has urban foxes. (South London has an awful lot of foxes, which are constantly turning over the bins. This is why it's such a good simile.)

Obviously you also have appetites or you wouldn't have read this far, and as you read on those appetites will only increase. You will want them sated. You will be desperate for ideas about what to eat, and I will give them to you. This is not a cookbook, designed to be kept in your kitchen, but it does include recipes – instructions for food that illustrate the points I'm making. There are one or two recipes per commandment, ideas that turn theoretical notions into something that makes sense on the plate rather than just on the page. It's the kind of cooking I actually do at home, rather than the aspirational stuff contained in all those glossy big-name cookbooks on your shelf which you thumb through from time to time but never actually use for fear of failure. Most of the recipes in this book are for things that don't make more washing-up than is strictly necessary, which I know is the kind of cooking you like. Not all of it is straightforward, because cooking isn't always easy or simple (see Commandment 4). But all of it is designed to satisfy appetites rather than intellectual curiosity.

For example, right now you need something to nibble on, something to keep you going as you turn the pages. So here's my recipe for pimped granola. I could call it muesli, but that makes it sound in some way healthy and this really isn't, even before you've added the nuggets of fudge and the chocolate chips.

JAY'S PIMPED GRANOLA

This makes over 1.5kg. Yes, that's a lot, but you have friends and you are desperate for them to like you. Plus this stuff is addictive. And if all else fails there's always Tupperware.

140g butter
250g demerara sugar
150g honey
100g golden syrup
zest of 1 orange
1 tsp vanilla essence
275g rolled oats (use jumbo oats if you can)
125g flaked almonds
190g mixed nuts (pecans, macadamias and cashews)
220g shredded or desiccated coconut
100g vanilla fudge, chopped
100g salted dark chocolate, chopped

- Preheat the oven to 170°C/325°F/gas 3.
- Gently heat the butter, sugar, honey, syrup, orange zest and vanilla essence in a pan until the sugar has dissolved.
- Mix the oats, nuts and coconut together.
- Pour the hot syrup mix over the dry ingredients and combine.
- Pour on to a tray lined with baking parchment. Make sure it's a flat, even spread and not too thick.
- Bake until golden, turning with a spatula every 5 minutes.
- Tip on to baking parchment.
- When it's cool enough to be handled, sprinkle over the fudge pieces and the chocolate chips.
- When it's finally cool, break up into pieces.

You like the sound of that, don't you? You really want to be eating it right now. In the old days you would have dispatched servants to go get the ingredients and bake it for you straight away. But who has servants any more? So either you go get the ingredients and make it yourself, or you buy some cheap substitute and eat that instead. It won't be the same, but at least it will stave off hunger as you read.

Although that is not one of my food commandments, it is *a* commandment.

Do as I say.

Thou shalt eat with thy hands

On 7 April 2015 the *Washington Post* ran a very important news story about Britain's general-election campaign. The headline read: 'Britain's prime minister ate a hot dog with a knife and fork, and it's a problem.'

Not for me it wasn't. The photograph of the incident merely confirmed everything I'd ever thought about the man. To me David Cameron had always looked like he would have sweaty palms on a cold winter's day; the sort who would let a beaming smile of welcome collapse into a grimace of utter disdain the moment you were out of sight. In short, he had always looked to me exactly like a politician.

Here was proof. It wasn't that I believed Cameron never ate hot dogs with his hands. Of course he did. Post the Pig-gate allegations – turn to Commandment 10 if you were asleep during September 2015 – I found myself more than capable of imagining Cameron doing lots of things with several of his extremities. It was that he simply didn't want to be *seen* eating hot dogs with his hands. He was at a 'family' barbecue, a staged visit on the campaign trail. Clearly he believed that if the electorate saw him touching his food with his fingers, they would immediately conclude that a man with such greasy digits – not to mention louche habits – should not be allowed anywhere near the nuclear button. If ever there has been an argument for eating with your hands, this is it. David Cameron is embarrassed about doing it, ergo you shouldn't be.

If it wasn't for the whole Pig-gate thing, this might have been a rule by which to live your life.

A willingness to eat with your hands is, for me, a signifier. I have long had an intense emotional relationship with spare ribs, for example; they are generally my answer to the death-row-meal question. Bring me a plate of those, hold the forks, and I won't exactly die happy, but I will at least be distracted from my impending death by the business of eating them. If ever I see someone eating spare ribs with a knife and fork – and I have – I get intensely angry. I know that if the two of us were to sit and talk, about anything at all, we would almost certainly have to be restrained from coming to blows. Our whole approach to life will be so completely different that it couldn't be otherwise. Someone like that does not deserve spare ribs. Give them to me.

I have always been this way. As a child, I was the one given the bone at table: the chicken wing, with its generous surface area, the better for the bronzed skin to crisp and bubble; the thick bone at the back of the roast rib of beef with the last tangle of pink meat and the crisped ribbons of fat; the curious, hard ankle on the leg of lamb with its overcoat of skin that I punctured with my teeth so that the juices could run. None of these things can be eaten with a knife and fork, or at least not efficiently. All of them yield up the good stuff, but only if your jaw is directly involved. Yes, your fingers get greasy and your cheeks smeared with juices, but that's what napkins were invented for.

At the time, I imagine my parents thought that, as I was so little and so clumsy with eating irons, it was easier to let me get hands-on. For me it was something much more primal, and it still is. Cutlery simply gets in the way. It gets between me and my dinner, and it gets between you and yours. When I eat with my hands I am inside my food, a joyous part of it. Now that I'm a father I am forever trying to instil in my own kids a certain dignity and decorum, an understanding that out there, beyond the hard, defined edges of our private family kitchen table, various kinds of behaviour will be expected. That behaviour does not include taking roast potatoes from the bowl to your mouth by hand, or picking at the salad with your fingers. As with so much of parenting I am, of course, a bloody hypocrite, because I am capable of all this and so much more. Stuff the banality of fish and chips, of burgers and hot dogs and those spare ribs. I'm not sure I've met a food that couldn't be eaten with fingers, and improved by doing so.

Ripping the parson's nose off the roast chicken before it gets anywhere near the table is entry-level stuff. A middle and index finger can do amazing things with a bowl of risotto – they make a pretty effective tool – and can also bring the comforting taste of your own skin to the party. All shellfish, whether hot or cold, in shell or out, are intensely tactile. So are roasted vegetables and salads and soup. Of course soup: just pick up the bloody bowl. And ice cream: there is true delight in the heat of your mouth warming the chilled tips of your fingers as you lick away the mess, although I accept this only really works with soft Italian-style gelato or something extruded from a van with the words 'Mr Whippy' emblazoned on the side.

Or 'the good ice cream', as it's known.

The idea of there being virtue in the experience of hot mouth on cold skin is not fanciful. The fact is that when you eat with your hands you are bringing the sense of touch into play along-side that of taste and smell. Charles Spence, Professor of Psychology at Oxford University and author of *The Perfect Meal: The Multisensory Science of Food and Dining*, is clear it has a major impact. 'Already we know that the feel of the texture in the hand can change [the] perceived texture of food in [the] mouth when people eat half fresh/half stale bagels,' he says, though he adds, 'More work has to be done.'

In her 1991 book, *The Rituals of Dinner*, the journalist, writer and broadcaster Margaret Visser goes further. 'To people who eat with their fingers,' she writes, 'hands seem cleaner, warmer, more agile than cutlery. Hands are silent, sensitive to texture and temperature, and graceful – providing, of course, that they have been properly trained.' Amen. I spend an awful lot of time training mine. As Spence explains in his book, there is evidence that when you eat with your hands, you eat less. A knife and fork – especially a fork – are such efficient instruments that you can simply shovel away, in a mechanical action, from elbow to wrist to mouth, which has its own compelling rhythm. Using your hands forces you to concentrate on what you're doing, to look at your plate and examine exactly what's going on down there. If this thought does not interest you, then you are simply not greedy enough. Put this book down. Go find something else to do. Take up woodwork.

Today we tend to regard the use of cutlery, and the kind used, as a mark of sophistication. It was not always this way. While there's evidence of spoons fashioned from shells and animal horns right from the very cradle days of human civilization, for a very long time the cutlery drawer in the Western world depended mostly on the knife, for cutting off lumps of what was wanted. (According to the California Academy of Sciences, which houses the Rietz Collection of Food Technology, East Asia has had chopsticks in one form or another for about 5,000 years.) The fork, the mother and father of all modern cutlery, is first documented during the Byzantine Empire, according to Spence. St Peter Damian, a hermit and ascetic, laid into the Venetian princess Maria Argyra specifically because she used one. 'Such was the luxury of her habits,' he wrote, that 'she deigned [not] to touch her food with her fingers, but would command her eunuchs to cut it up into small pieces, which she would impale on a certain golden instrument with two prongs and thus carry to her mouth.' The woman had eunuchs, for God's sake. Of course she refused to eat with her hands. As another member of the clergy present at the dinner put it (as quoted by Chad Ward in an article on the website Leite's Culinaria), 'God in his wisdom has provided man with natural forks – his fingers. Therefore it is an insult to him to substitute artificial metal forks for them when eating.'

Bugger God; it's just nowhere near as fun.

The fork did not arrive in Europe until the 1630s, and did not become broadly popular until the nineteenth century. Louis XIV, whose reign saw its arrival, banned his children from eating with them, and the English aristocracy regarded them as effeminate. Unfortunately, I recognize that the homophobia of the English aristocracy undermines my argument somewhat; if it was seen as a bad thing by people who gained their wealth solely because of whose vagina they came out of, then we should probably all be for it.

Then again, the enemy of your enemy need not always be your friend. Happily some big-name chefs now agree with me. Just a few years ago, at his Los Angeles restaurant A-Frame, Korean-American chef Roy Choi was actively encouraging his customers not to use cutlery. 'You eat with conviction and passion when using your hands,' he told The *New York Times* in 2012. 'I hope that people let their guard down and throw out some of the rules we have regarding etiquette and connect like animals.'

A few years before that, in 2007, a Danish chef called René Redzepi put a dish of rough-cut steak tartar with sorrel leaves, crushed juniper and a tarragon emulsion on the menu at his restaurant Noma, on the Copenhagen quayside. The idea was that you used the sharp bitter leaves to sweep up the raw beef by hand. In time, as Noma rose to the top of the controversial 'World's 50 Best Restaurants' list, Redzepi would become famed for his insistence that his food stick rigidly to a regional agenda. He believed that as his was a Northern European restaurant, it should eschew the Mediterranean fripperies of olive oil and olives, sun-dried tomatoes and the like in favour of butter and bitter greens. The rough stone-walled dining room, with bare wood tables and pelts thrown over seats, felt like a conscious effort to channel his Viking forebears. But it was the steak tartar dish, to be eaten by hand, that drew the most attention.

'When Noma first opened, this dish almost seemed a provocation,' I was told by the British food writer Michael Booth, who has lived in Denmark for over a decade and has been eating at the restaurant almost since it launched in 2004. 'The Copenhagen restaurant scene really was dominated by these old, fussy French places. And then along comes this restaurant where they want you to eat raw beef with your hands like you're some Viking.' Restaurants at this level – it eventually acquired two Michelin stars – don't generally do away with the cutlery. The *LA Times* called it a classic. Frank Bruni of The *New York Times* simply described the whole hands-on business as 'great theatre' and 'a lot of fun'.

For Redzepi himself it was simply about rejecting the old order. 'When we first put it on the menu, he says now, 'I was consciously trying to find ways to take the edge off the formal dining experience. At that time it was all about real silverware and fine linens. I grew up in a time where there was a tool for every act of eating, and the better you were as a restaurant the fancier the metal. So it was a reaction against that. It surprised people a lot back then. Today it's more common.'

This is what we call progress.

One afternoon, I go to see my friend Daniel Bexfield, one of London's leading dealers in fine silver, and an expert on cutlery in particular. He owns and runs the Silver Spoon Club of Great Britain, publishes their magazine, the *Finial*, and has a fabulous shop tucked away in Cecil Court off London's Charing Cross Road. It's full of glass cabinets packed with shine and sparkle and curve. I'd heard he owned a spoon that had belonged to four British monarchs. If anyone can convince me that cutlery improves the experience of dinner, it's Daniel.

I ask him what it is about cutlery of the sort he deals in that appeals to him. 'If you have a beautiful object in your hand it improves the experience,' he says. 'I just think there's something very satisfying about eating with an object of quality.' Professor Charles Spence would nod sagely at this. There is much evidence, Spence says, that we value an eating experience more if the tools used to experience it have weight and heft. So if you want your friends to think you're a much better cook than you actually are, give them a really heavy silver knife and fork with which to eat it. Yes, we really are that simple.

Daniel fetches the spoon of which I have heard so much. It dates from 1729, and was made by silversmith Caleb Hill of London as part of a whole canteen that would probably have run to eighty-four pieces. It is made of solid silver but gilded using a process involving mercury mixed with gold. The mercury is then burned off to leave the honeyed golden layer. There is a clearly defined hallmark along the handle, and the royal crest on the finial at the end.

'This spoon was made for George II, and then inherited by George III, George IV and William IV, at which point Queen Victoria came to the throne.' As a woman she could not take the title of King of Hanover. That went to the fifth son of George III, who turned out to be a bit of a thief. 'He took without permission a whole array of royal silver of which this spoon was a part,' Daniel says 'There's documentation of Queen Vic writing to him and asking for it all back.'

Around 1911 the collection was sold, and this spoon began changing hands until it landed here in Cecil Court. Normally an item of this sort would be worth £200, but because of the royal connections Daniel values it at north of £2,000. There is no doubting the craftsmanship. It is a beautiful object, and the provenance adds to the allure. You can't help but look at it and wonder whose fingertips have brushed its surface. But I don't find myself craving a bowl of soup to dip it into.

I ask Daniel if he likes eating with his hands. 'Fish and chips,' he says. 'I like eating those with my fingers, but . . .' Yes? 'The Ivy has spare ribs on the menu now but I won't order them,' he says, mentioning the famed London theatreland restaurant, where he is a regular. I ask him why not. 'It's messy and sticky. In any restaurant I wouldn't have a burger either because I don't want to eat that with my hands.' So it's about context? 'Yes, it's about context. It's not about being snobby. It's just that if I eat with my fingers I want to be able to lick them and in a restaurant I couldn't.'

Finally we have identified the differences between me and Daniel Bexfield.

He owns a spoon once owned by four monarchs. I do not.

He will not lick his fingers in polite company. I don't care who I lick my fingers with.

Clearly I am a terrible, terrible man. But I am happy.

A few years ago I went to Tokyo in search of the very best things to eat. Through a contact I arranged to have dinner at a tiny high-end restaurant called Okei-Sushi. Normally it served only six. Tonight the entire blonde wood bar was just for me. I could bang on about the perfect pieces of gastronomic art fashioned for me from raw fish and rice by sushi master Masashi Suzuki that night: the sashimi of red snapper dressed with lime, the curls of raw clam with ponzu and soy, the unagi and the bream and the octopus. All of it was glorious.

But what really stayed with me was the lesson in how to eat nigiri sushi. Japanese manners and codes of conduct are so complex that I was told by one Japanese chef I shouldn't even bother trying to get to grips with them, not least because no Japanese person would ever expect me to. I had, however, always assumed that sushi was to be eaten delicately with chopsticks. Mr Suzuki put me right. Forget chopsticks. This was a job for hands. Roll each piece on to its back with your middle finger, then pick up between thumb and index finger. Tip your head back and place the sushi on your tongue fish down.

Of course you couldn't do this with chopsticks. It would be

impossible. My fingertips were so much more precise. Plus they were warm and sensitive. They were the perfect tools for the job.

That was the light-bulb moment. If something as complex and sophisticated as the best sushi in the world was to be eaten with your hands, what couldn't be? And if eating with your hands actively improved the experience, why wouldn't you? Of course cutlery has its place. A fork is very efficient and sometimes lunch really is just fuel, even for me. And of course sometimes there might not be an easy way to clean your hands. But in the perfect circumstances, and even the imperfect ones, there is nothing more satisfying than shoving the metalwork to one side, rolling up your sleeves and getting down to it, one animal's skin to another.

You know it makes sense.

Food for Eating with Your Hands

EGG, ONION AND ANCHOVY

This is a riff on the Ashkenazi Jewish staple of egg and onion, and is best eaten by being scooped straight out of the bowl using crackers. It's a brilliant thing to put in the middle of the table at the beginning of dinner, though it never lasts long.

Serves 6–8 as canapés

4 eggs
4 spring onions, finely chopped
2 tins of salted anchovies (the really good Spanish type if
    you can afford them, but any will do), roughly chopped
a handful of fresh flat-leaf parsley, finely chopped
ground black pepper

For the vinaigrette

100ml olive oil
75ml white wine vinegar
2 tsp Dijon mustard
2 tsp mayonnaise
a good pinch of sea salt

- Place the eggs in a pan of cold water and bring to the boil. Cook for 3 minutes, then remove from the pan and allow to cool. Peel them, then crush them with a fork in a bowl as if making egg mayonnaise (which, to be honest, you almost are).
- Add the spring onions, the anchovies and the flat-leaf parsley. Mix it all together.
- Put the ingredients for the vinaigrette into an old jam jar that you have retained for the purpose, tighten the lid and shake vigorously for a minute or so until emulsified. You are making a basic mustardy dressing, so now

it's down to taste. If you find it too sharp, add more mayonnaise. If it's not sharp enough, add a dribble more vinegar. This will probably make more vinaigrette than you need, but it's hard to make less. Keep the remainder for a salad.

- Add half the vinaigrette to the egg mixture and fork over again. Add more if you want it sharper. Finally, add a good grind of black pepper.

CHICKEN WINGS WITH LEMON, GARLIC AND FENNEL SEED

It might be possible to eat these utterly compelling wings with a knife and fork, but I don't think I'd enjoy watching anyone try. They are all about the hands, though to make it practical the wings must be jointed, not least because unjointed wings cook unevenly. The holy trinity of lemon, garlic and fennel seeds works brilliantly with many other things, and especially on pork.

Serves 6–8, depending on greed

2kg jointed chicken wings, the tips discarded (or kept for stock)
4 fat cloves of garlic, crushed with the flat blade of a knife, then chopped
juice of 1 lemon
4 tbsp fennel seeds
2 tsp sea salt
4 tbsp olive oil

- Preheat the oven to 200°C/400°F/gas 6.
- Combine all the ingredients in a bowl, turning the wings with your hands (but of course) to coat them evenly. You can then store them in the fridge for a few hours if you wish.

- Put on to an oven tray in a single layer. For this volume of wings you may need two trays.
- Shove in the oven for an hour. After 45 minutes, check the wings. If they're browned on top, turn them over, making sure to scrape up seeds and garlic from the bottom of the tray. At this point do not be afraid of turning the oven up to 220°C/425°F/gas 7 to finish them off. You want them brown, the skin bubbled, the fennel seeds crisp.
- If nobody's watching you can eat them straight out of the tray, or you can pile them up in serving bowls, but either way leave them to cool for 10 to 15 minutes so you can eat them without burning your fingers.
- Put a bowl in the middle of the table for the bones. And some kitchen roll for fingers.

2.

Thou shalt always worship leftovers

Leftovers are the neglected stepchild of the food world, the lunch option too many people would prefer to pretend does not exist. If something was not the intended outcome, if it was not the reason for cooking in the first place, how can it be any good? Very easily.

Never does this strike me more than when I'm at a dinner party. Or, to be more exact, when I'm throwing one.

The fact is I don't get invited to dinner parties, not any more. Very few people are willing to cook for a man who earns a living standing in judgement on other people's kitchen efforts. My wife says this is probably for the best; that I only come away from a night at someone else's table grumbling like an old man with untreated piles.

'But I never criticize anyone's food to their face, or ever actually.'

'No, you don't. You make me listen to it all in the car on the way home.'

I protest about only really being interested in the chance to sit down with friends, but I know it's academic. Apart from a couple of very old mates who don't so much invite us to dinner parties as simply announce they're cooking food for the family as usual and would we like to pop over, the invitations do not come. So instead we have to issue them.

I like feeding people. I like a big cooking project and I like filling their plates with the end result. It makes me happy. But even as I'm doing so, even as I'm sliding the heavy spoon through, say, a shoulder of lamb that's been braising for so long that using a knife to serve it would be classed as an act of overengineering, I am hoping they don't eat it all. (See recipe at the end.) Because what I'm looking at is not tonight's star dish for them. I'm looking at tomorrow's fabulous leftover opportunities for me. Braised shoulder of lamb, which has surrendered all its tension to a hot liquor of red wine and chorizo and brown sugar, is an utter joy fresh from the oven. But the next day there are even better things to be had. Lumps of the fridge-cold meat with their hard white overcoat of fat can be thrown into a fiercely hot pan until all of it is crisp and brown. The crunch of sea salt, a smear of nose-tickling mustard, and life is very good indeed.

I'm like this at Christmas too. Of course excess roast potatoes crushed and shattered with cabbage become bubble and squeak, because that's the law. To do otherwise would be wrong. But there are other things. On Christmas Eve I glaze a huge ham in honey and mustard and soy – a bigger piece than my family could ever hope to eat as cold cuts – and roast it fiercely until it's the colour of a lacquered Chinese box. I'm excited about eating it simply in slices as it cools, and perhaps for the few days that follow. But after that it's time for thick slabs to go into the pan until they're the colour of copper kitchen pans, to be eaten with fried eggs. Cubes of it are braised in chicken stock, the meaty liquor then poured into a béchamel to make a glorious sauce to bind it all together. Into a casserole dish it goes, under a puff pastry lid, for its twenty-minute journey through the hot oven, and the world settles comfortably on its axis. And when you get down to the bone, with those barnacles of meat that won't easily slice away, there is soup to be made, until the ham has given its all. You get the point: the leftovers are why you embark on a major cooking exercise in the first place.

There is only one problem with leftovers. It's the word 'leftovers'.

It speaks of expediency and second best. The *New Yorker* magazine writer Calvin Trillin once claimed that the most remarkable thing about his mother was that 'for thirty years she served the family nothing but leftovers. The original meal has never been found.' Ruth Reichl, former restaurant critic of *The New York Times*, decried her mother as the creator of 'dreadful concoctions. She really prided herself on something called "Everything Stew", where she would take everything in the refrigerator, all the leftovers, and put them all together.' The knowingness is not simply about the quality of the food but of the cook. We are meant to think of all mothers as brilliant cooks, because it's a part of the job description. They nurture, ergo they sauté. And roast. And braise. And bake. To admit your mother was not any good in the kitchen, even with the lightest of 'what can you do?' shrugs, is to subvert the culture. And how better to do it than through leftovers, the edible butt of every hungry joke?

It was not always this way. In her 2015 article for the *Atlantic*, Helen Veit, an associate professor of history at Michigan State University, explained that in nineteenth-century America the food not eaten at the meal for which it was originally cooked wasn't thought of as a separate thing. It was just all food, the uneaten there to continue feeding you for days to come. The closest a cookbook got to the modern idea of leftovers was the use of the French term *réchauffé*, meaning 'reheated'. Breakfast, for example, would have been dependent on whatever had been cooked in the crock pot for the night before, a hit of carbs and protein designed to sustain you through the agricultural labour in which most of the population were engaged. This was the age before refrigeration. It was therefore incumbent on the household, when presented with excess food, to press into service whatever preservation techniques were to hand, be it smoking, pickling, potting (in melted butter), salting or fermenting. Likewise, while it's easy to see cheese simply as a product separate from the prime ingredient required for its manufacture, it should be considered in terms of surplus. If you ran a dairy in the nineteenth century, cheese was not merely an end in itself. It was a way of using up excess milk, just as spirits, beer and wines were a way of making sure that excess grains and grapes could live on to a great and useful old age. All of these foodstuffs were made both for later and to last. Back in the nineteenth century the very term 'leftover' would not have been recognized.

The rot set in when refrigeration arrived in middle-class homes in the US at the start of the twentieth century, much earlier than it did in Britain, where the middle classes had to wait until the 1950s. Where once you had to find ways to preserve excess ingredients before they were cooked, now last night's dinner went into the fridge, heading back out to the table repeatedly, in roughly the same guise. As Veit points out, one of the first cookbooks to use the term was entitled *Left-Over Foods and How to Use Them*, and was paid for by a company that made fridges. It did not appear until 1910.

The British story of excess food is different. It's longer and defined, like so much else in British life, by class hierarchies. In America, it was all about individual families looking after themselves on the farmsteads. In Britain, it was all about the nobility looking after the poor by passing on the excess. Of course, for a nobleman, having more on the table than he, his family and his entourage could possibly eat was a mark of status and achievement. Walking away from a table of uneaten food was an efficient way of proving you were a man of means. But it was also a way of both maintaining the household and giving patronage to others. In the medieval and Tudor periods, for example, the pastry under which the contents of pies were baked was rarely eaten by the family of the house, but passed over to their servants. According to the food historian Dr Annie Gray, this giving away of surplus food also went beyond that to the surrounding communities living on the lord's land.

'The big house had a responsibility for keeping the poor fed,' she says. 'By passing over their excess. It's a kind of edible alms-giving which goes on until the creation of the welfare state after the Second World War. Certainly the excess was not regarded as waste.' In that context the food bank, the shelves filled by the concerned middle classes for those less fortunate than themselves, should no longer be seen as a modern aberration. The first may have opened in Phoenix, Arizona, in 1967, before spreading to Europe in the 1980s and then to Britain in 2000 where, by the last count, there are now over 440; but in truth they are just a return to a bleak, depressing historical norm.

In the middle-class homes of Victorian Britain, having a large roast on a Sunday which could not be finished that day was not just a mark of status, but also a supply of the week's meals, there to be recycled into cold cuts, stews and soups throughout the week, and to be fed to the servants. This wasn't leftovers. This was simply lunch. The great Mrs Beeton was responsible for very few original recipes. At best she can be credited with collecting other people's work; at worst she can be fingered for theft. But one of those that *was* hers was a version of shepherd's pie in which the roast lamb or mutton was minced with chopped onions and placed in a pie dish between layers of potato. (Intriguingly, well over a century later Michel Roux Jr, the head chef of Le Gavroche in London, was asked by the BBC for a family recipe using leftovers. He described a version of shepherd's pie made by his mother which used the minced roast leg of lamb from the day before.) Likewise, in Victorian cookery books there are endless recipes designed for using bread that is past its best: not just in bread-and-butter or summer puddings, but as the bulk for stuffings and sausages, and for putting a crumb coating on almost anything edible. Extra bread was not merely something that had been left over, but a necessary household ingredient.

Excess food in the home only really started being regarded as a negative after the Second World War, when growing efficiencies in farming meant an increasing abundance of food and a marked drop in its cost. In 1900, families were on average spending 50 per cent of their available income on keeping themselves fed. When it cost that much, you simply couldn't be extravagant or casual. Waste was a serious issue. After the Second World War, that proportion dropped dramatically, hitting 20 per cent of income by 1970 and 10 per cent today. With food now so cheap, who cares if you scrape the waste into the bin at the end of the meal? It was post-war that leftovers began to occupy their current position of second best, more so in some countries than others. In the post-war edition of *Larousse Gastronomique*, the French culinary bible, there is only one recipe among the thousands which can be described as utilizing leftovers. It is for 'reheated lamb' and reads thus:

> Cut cold, cooked shoulder or leg of lamb into very thin slices and arrange on a lightly buttered dish. Coat with one of the following boiling hot sauces: bordelaise, bourguignonne, charcutiere, chasseur, duxelles, Italian, lyonnaise, Madeira or poivrade. Cover and reheat gently on the top of the stove or in a bain-marie.

As a Gallic shrug of disdain it's hard to imagine anything better. Leftovers? Well, if you really must. Just find some meat and drown it in any old sauce you happen to have to hand. If you want something made with the stuff that's left behind, go talk to those uncouth Italians or Spanish.

After all, the Italians have credibility in the leftover stakes, with the much-revered arancini being possible only if you have leftover cold risotto to be formed into balls and deep-fried; likewise Spanish croquetas – a flavoured béchamel sauce, chilled to solid, breadcrumbed and deep-fried – are a vehicle for the smallest pieces of cured ham left on the bone when the rest has been cut away.

But the wheel of history is turning. Still we have refrigeration. Still we have abundance, at least for now. However, we also have climate change and a debate about environmental impact and sustainability. The volume of food wasted in the Western world is a disgrace. We waste more food in North America and Europe every year than is produced in the whole of sub-Saharan Africa. The British alone waste 7.2 million tonnes of food a year, enough to fill Wembley Stadium to the brim seven times over. We spend £12.5 billion a year on this food, or around £680 for every family with children in the country. Indeed, it's not only a waste of food; it's a familiar waste. You've probably heard these statistics before. But it's not just the money: there's all the embedded carbon and water required to produce it. The overfed world's wasted food is one huge, avoidable and utterly pointless carbon footprint.

Unless we eat it.

So now leftovers are not simply a source of the good stuff; they bring with them a moral imperative too. As history has shown us, excess food should simply be thought of as an ingredient rather than something left behind. It's the way serious restaurants do it. In a restaurant, every ounce of food thrown away is profit in the landfill. 'Nothing should ever go in the bin,' says Michel Roux Jr. 'It's not just about peelings or bones into the stock pot. It's about thinking in a joined-up way about ingredients.' It's why he came up with the scraps challenge for *Masterchef: The Professionals*, which he presented for the BBC until 2013. 'I asked for the scraps challenge to be put in years ago. The producers kept refusing. They simply said it wasn't good enough telly.' Oh, how wrong they were: seeing a young cook panic when faced by a cod's head, a set of beef bones clad in everyone else's leavings, and what they might consider to be the wrong end of the asparagus, is a joy to behold. It's only the skilled ones who spot the cod cheeks, ripe for sautéing with a little butter and garlic, the beef that can be braised and re-formed into deep-fried croquettes, the perfect-if-humble makings of an asparagus mousse. That's the thing. Leftovers force you to think creatively, to fashion greatness from the mundane. On the back of a chicken, for example, is a small lozenge of meat called the oyster. In French it is called *sot-l'y-laisse*, which roughly translates as 'the piece the idiot leaves behind'. Nobody wants to be that idiot.

Nobody wants to leave anything behind, especially if it's the good stuff. When cooking with excess, one recipe leads to another in a game of gastronomic tag. And sometimes a dish that happened by accident is so good that it becomes a solid part of the repertoire, in ways you never expected. Examples of this are included in the recipes that follow. Start thinking like this, and the food you put on the table for lunch or dinner is not the end of the process. It's just the beginning.

The Original Dish

BRAISED SHOULDER OF LAMB

Serves 6

2–2.5kg shoulder of lamb
3 tbsp olive oil
flaky sea salt and ground black pepper
1 large onion, roughly chopped
2 cooking chorizo sausages, or half a chorizo ring, sliced
3 fat cloves of garlic, crushed with the flat blade of a knife,
    then chopped
½ a bottle of reasonable red wine
1 litre chicken stock (from cubes is fine)
2 tbsp brown sugar
runny honey

- Preheat the oven to 170°C/325°F/gas 3.
- Meanwhile, heat a deep roasting tin big enough to take
  the whole shoulder of lamb on the stove top. Pour in the
  oil. Season the lamb shoulder liberally with the sea salt
  and black pepper, and brown on all sides. This is a
  lengthy job and will require you to stand over it, tipping
  the piece of meat this way and that with tongs to make
  sure it's as well browned as possible. Don't be too
  obsessive. Just some colour is good. When done, remove
  from the roasting tin to a plate.
- Add the onion and the chorizo and cook until caramelized,
  then add the garlic and cook for a minute more.
- Pour in the red wine to deglaze, scraping away at any
  bits on the bottom. Boil on a high heat for 2 minutes to
  burn off the alcohol.
- Top up with the chicken stock, throw in the brown
  sugar and stir.

- Return the lamb shoulder to the pan. The liquor should cover it by at least half. If it's a particularly square, deep piece, add another half litre of stock.
- Cover the whole tin with foil and place in the oven for 4 hours. Check it's cooked by sticking two forks into the meat and pulling them apart. The meat should come away easily. If not, return to the oven for another half an hour.
- Carefully strain the liquor into a pan, and place over a moderate heat. Cook until the liquor has reduced by two-thirds, then adjust the seasoning to taste. You now have your gravy. Indeed, you'll have far too much. I suggest you freeze some for another day and another dish.
- Meanwhile, drizzle the lamb with the runny honey. Turn the oven on to grill, and return the meat to the oven, basting after 5 minutes with any honey that dribbles off. After 10 minutes it should be dark and sticky.
- Sprinkle with some more sea salt and rest for a good 20 minutes.

The Leftovers

If your crowd eat all of the lamb, bad luck. Otherwise cut what remains off the bone and store in the fridge overnight. It will keep for a good three days like this, and will fry off beautifully in a very hot frying pan. Perfect in sandwiches or with salad. Or just eat it out of the cooling pan while standing by the stove. I won't judge you.

The Original Dish

This is a quick pasta dish which I had been making for years before I realized the leftover potential in the bottom of the serving bowl. In truth, with this one, the original dish simply became the jumping-off point for another dish entirely. It's that kind of happenstance which makes the kitchen such a fun place.

TAGLIATELLE WITH CLAMS AND BACON

Serves 4

500g live clams or mussels
2 tbsp olive oil
100g smoked lardons or chopped streaky bacon
¼ tsp chilli flakes
2 cloves of garlic, crushed with the flat blade of a knife and
   chopped
½ a bottle of good dry white wine
250g dried egg pasta such as tagliatelle (the good stuff that
   cooks in less than 5 minutes)
a handful of fresh flat-leaf parsley, chopped

- Put the clams or mussels through two changes of cold
  water, picking out any that have cracked shells (and
  debeard the mussels). Drain them from the water in a
  colander just before you start cooking.
- Put on a pan of boiling water big enough for the pasta.
- In a deep-sided frying pan, heat the oil. Add the lardons
  or bacon and cook until they start to crisp.
- Add the chilli flakes, using a wooden spoon to make
  sure they are evenly spread. Turn on the extractor fan or
  open the window, because even that small of amount of
  chilli will make you cough. Add the garlic and continue
  frying for 30 seconds.
- Pour in just half a glass of the wine to the very hot
  pan at first, which will immediately boil furiously.
  Scrape away at the bottom of the pan to pick up
  anything there. Once the boil has subsided, add the

rest of the wine. (If you add it all straight away it's likely to flame as the wine spits on to the burner, which is fun if you like that sort of thing, but to be avoided if you don't.)

- Let the alcohol cook off for a minute, then add the shellfish, and put as big a saucepan lid over the top as you can, so they steam in the liquor. Lift the lid occasionally and shove the shellfish around so they all have space to open. It should take 3 to 5 minutes, depending on their size.
- Put on the pasta. Cook until al dente, then drain.
- Warm a serving bowl. Add the pasta, pour on the clam, lardon and wine mixture, then throw in the chopped flat-leaf parsley and mix together.
- Eat.

The Leftovers

One night, after making the pasta dish, I noticed in the bottom of the serving bowl a good pint of the liquor that had been left behind. I gave it a taste. It was fabulous: a deep rich fishy stock from the clams, but with the added bonus of the wine, the garlic, the bacon and of course the chilli. It was too good to waste. In time I began making this broth from scratch (see instructions on page 25), but this time I just put it in the fridge for the next day.

A KIND OF HOT AND SOUR ASIAN NOODLE SOUP

This recipe is easily scalable, though watch the amount of chilli flakes and adjust according to taste. You can also throw in almost any seafood you like, including clams, mussels and, best of all, raw king scallops sliced thinly. If you want more heat, a couple of drops of Tabasco does the trick.

Serves 2

450ml leftover liquor from the pasta (see page 23)
450ml chicken stock (from a cube is fine)
1 clove of garlic, finely sliced
a thumb-sized piece of fresh ginger, peeled and sliced into
    batons
2 spring onions, finely sliced
1 lemon
fish sauce (optional)
200g fine egg noodles (roughly half a standard pack)
150–200g peeled king prawns, raw if possible
1 tbsp sesame oil
a handful of fresh coriander

- Strain the liquor from the pasta into a saucepan and bring
  to a simmer. Add the stock and bring back to a simmer.
- Now add the garlic, ginger, spring onions, the finely
  sliced peel of ¼ of the lemon, and a squeeze of lemon
  juice. We're basically turning our Italian pasta broth into
  a hot and sour Asian broth. If you want it fishier and
  saltier, add a tablespoon of nam pla, or fish sauce.
- Let it simmer for 5 minutes on a low heat.
- Add the noodles, separating with chopsticks, then
  immediately add the raw prawns. If the prawns are
  already cooked, wait a minute or so before adding as
  you only want to heat them through.
- Cook the noodles for 3 minutes, then dress the soup
  with the sesame oil and serve in a deep bowl, sprinkled
  with the fronds of fresh coriander.

TO MAKE THE BROTH FROM SCRATCH

2 tbsp olive oil
100g smoked lardons or chopped streaky bacon

1 tsp dried shrimp paste (available from Asian
supermarkets)
¼ teaspoon chilli flakes
½ a bottle of moderately good white wine
1 litre chicken stock (from cubes is fine)

- Heat the oil in a deep saucepan and fry the lardons or bacon until they start to crisp.
- Add the shrimp paste and the chilli flakes. Stir the shrimp paste into the oil for a couple of minutes, so it cooks out.
- Pour the wine into the pan to deglaze, scraping up any bits that stick on the bottom with your wooden spoon, then pour in the stock and simmer for 3 minutes. There will be no leftovers.

3.

Thou shalt covet thy neighbour's oxen

Back in 1994 a wannabe chef from London went on a culinary pilgrimage to Brittany. He often did things like this. He had spent most of his twenties working dead-end jobs – as a credit controller, as a bailiff – simply to pay for such trips, which he was certain would help improve the small restaurant he dreamed of opening. The trip to Brittany was just another one. 'I spent years back then trying to seek out the best of everything in food,' Heston Blumenthal says now. 'That trip, the last before I opened the Fat Duck, was to the town of Quiberon in Brittany to taste Monsieur Le Roux's caramels.'

It all sounds rather humble, doesn't it, verging on the preposterous. Who would bother getting on a ferry to another country just to try some caramels? Could any food item really be worth all that? But without those caramels and, more to the point, without Blumenthal's obsessive desire for them, his need to find out about a food item at its very source, our modern food landscape would be a rather less delightful place. For the man he went to see was a chocolatier called Henri Le Roux, and he was the inventor not just of a sweet or even of a collection of them, but of an entire flavour category.

He was the man who invented salted caramel.

Le Roux, the son of a cake-shop owner, moved to Brittany in the late 1970s, having trained as a chocolatier at the Coba Institute in Switzerland. He was looking for a product that might define his new shop and decided to take inspiration from the foods around him. Brittany had long been renowned for its sea salt, which found voice in the other great product of the region, its butter. The salted butter from Brittany is world famous in food circles. Wouldn't it be great, Le Roux thought, if he could use that in a sweet? The result was his soft, sweet-savoury salted butter caramels, with a flavour that seemed to go on long after the toffee had dissolved in your mouth. It was quickly a hit. That first year he sold nearly 400 kilos of the stuff. In 1980 the French trade association for confectioners named it their sweet of the year.

And yet for a long time it remained very much a local cult. If you were in Quiberon, you went to see Monsieur Le Roux and bought his caramels and raved about them to your friends. Perhaps you took a few home, but that was the extent of it.

It would have stayed that way were it not for people like Blumenthal, and their hunger for new flavours. The Danish sociologist and trends expert Henrik Vejlgaard has identified a process by which the rarefied and exotic, like salted caramel, becomes mainstream. Trends, Vejgaard says, emerge in seven cities around the world – New York, Los Angeles and San Francisco in the US, alongside London, Paris, Milan and Tokyo – because they are home to the greatest concentrations of 'trendsetters'. Those trendsetters, he says, come from distinct groups: artists and designers, people under the age of thirty, the wealthy, and gay men – which on the one hand looks like a lunge at the stereotyping of gay culture, but on the other hand really doesn't. 'A trendsetter,' Vejlgaard says, 'is someone who is constantly very curious about what is new and innovative. A trendsetter craves change.'

Our trendsetter sounds exhausting, but without people like that, we would never have been able to buy a bag of salted caramel toffee popcorn, or a Cornish sea salt caramel muffin, or a salted caramel KitKat. And who would want to live in a world like that?

Certainly Blumenthal fits the mould: no, he wasn't wealthy in any way, but he was under thirty, he was from London, and he is famously restless. In 1995 when he opened the Fat Duck in the Berkshire village of Bray, a small square block of salted butter caramel was on his menu as part of a dessert that mimicked breakfast. Back then it was very much a humble bistro with a few interesting cooking techniques going on in the background, rather than the modernist gastro-fantasy it is today, and yet that is one of the few original ideas still available. To this day he has a small square salted caramel in an edible wrapper on the menu, as part of the petits fours.

So salted caramel had found its way to London (or as near as damn it: Bray is just a few miles outside). In the late 1990s it was the turn of Paris, when the pâtissier Pierre Hermé introduced a salted caramel macaroon to the gourmands of the French capital, to rapturous applause (and also started sprinkling sea salt from Brittany on dark chocolate). Back in London, around the turn of the millennium, an Irish chocolatier called Gerard Coleman of Artisan du Chocolat was commissioned by the chef Gordon Ramsay to make chocolates with a centre of liquid salted caramel for his flagship restaurant in London's Chelsea. Meanwhile, over in New York, restaurants like the Gramercy Tavern and Le Cirque were sprinkling chocolate and caramel desserts with flakes of the finest sea salt.

It was ready to slip gently into the mainstream. In 2003 the Seattle-based firm Fran's Chocolates won an award from the National Association for the Speciality Food Trade for a salted caramel which famously would go on to receive the patronage of one Barack Obama. In 2004 a recipe for caramel with sea salt turned up in the US food magazine *Gourmet*. And if *Gourmet* thought it was a thing, well then, there was clearly money to be made from it. As reported by *The New York Times*, in April 2008 Häagen-Dazs launched a salted caramel flavour ice cream, followed six months later by Starbucks, who introduced salted caramel hot chocolate. For Christmas that year the flavour was included in a selection sold by Walmart.

And now? It's in every coffee shop and on most dessert menus. It flavours popcorn and biscuits. You can get salted caramel flavoured green tea from Twinings, which sounds like a terrible idea, and salted caramel tequila or vodka, which doesn't sound much better. In December 2015 the discount supermarket chain Aldi introduced a salted caramel and bourbon ham joint to its British stores. The *BBC Good Food Magazine* chose the ham as a top pick for Christmas because it had 'the right balance between sweet and salty'. What had started as a sweet idea, with a hint of savoury, was now a savoury idea that needed a hint of sweet. Salted caramel was officially everywhere.

It's a story repeated time and again. It's the story of both American barbecue and dirty burgers across Britain. It's the story of Korean chicken wings, the crisp batter drenched in an utterly compelling hot red chilli sauce, and of Dominique Ansel's Cronuts – half croissant, half doughnut, all cult object. We eat, therefore we covet. Therefore food ideas spread.

According to Moses, all this covetousness makes us terrible people. It pollutes our minds. If so I have been an awful person since I was a small boy. This is because my soul has always been blackened by dreadful food lusts.

My first lustful memory is of being a six-year-old boy in a London restaurant with my older brother and sister and my parents. It was a fancy place, the sort where food moved around the room on trolleys, and waiters regularly set fire to things. The room smelled of alcohol being burned off, of hot sugar and browned butter. It smelled good.

I have no recollection of what was on my plate. Probably a small steak that had been incinerated, for I was young and stupid and knew no better. The distinct memory is of what was on another table in front of someone else. It was clearly a complicated business. The diner had a dimpled dish before him, each of the six holes filled with a shell spiralled in shades of brown and beige. In one hand he held shiny, chromium tongs with belled ends. In the other he held a pick. He was eating snails – escargot, of course, because this would have been the earliest months of the 1970s when in England the original French still held sway – and it looked like huge fun. It looked exactly like the sort of fun a six-year-old boy with a commitment to appetite would enjoy. Or at least this six-year-old boy.

I made my case. My parents looked at each other and shrugged. The snails were ordered. I went to work and discovered I was right. I did love them, even though, at first, I found the tongs hard to manage. The instinct to squeeze once you had a shell in hold, its black hole facing you, was very strong indeed. But if you did that, the shell dropped out. Quickly I learned the wrist action, and came to adore the process of probing and pulling, and the fat, black, garlic-butter-drenched punctuation marks that this delivered up. And then I got to discard the tools altogether, and pick up the cooling shells with my hands – but of course – and probe for the salty crusted bits of garlic and parsley with my tongue. It was bliss. I coveted those snails something rotten and I got them.

So am I really such a bad man? Likewise, was Blumenthal such an awful person for coveting the taste of salted caramel?

Let's look at it another way. What has been the greatest driver of global food culture? There are various contenders of the blunt, mechanistic variety. You could credit global trade, for without the trading of spice how would we have brought flavour to our food in the New World? Then again, if you start bigging up the spice trade, you also have to accept the influence of colonialism in general and the slave trade in particular, both of which all too often had a symbiotic relationship with it. Slaves were regularly swapped for spices, and the slave trade often helped fund and justify the various legs of the journey. There's refrigeration of course, which certainly expanded the lifespan of foods, though, as we know, the main impact of that was to give leftovers a bad name. We could look to advances in agriculture. There is no doubt that farming was a driver of human civilization; that once we were able to stop foraging, we were left with much more time on our hands to develop cave painting, prose poetry and latte art. But agriculture has always had mass production as its imperative rather than diversity.

That said, the extra time that developments in agriculture gifted us does have a role to play. For, when it comes to food culture, the biggest driver of change is not a process. It's not a technological development. It's an emotion.

That emotion is boredom: with what's on your plate, not just right now, but last night and for nights to come. It's the desire for something more interesting to eat; for life not to stay the same. This is one of those things that separate us from other animals. Give them a good, balanced and appropriate diet and most of the animal kingdom will be happy to eat the same thing day in, day out. Indeed, they may depend upon it. Give that to humans and we'd go quietly, and then very noisily, mad. We crave variety because we need stimulation, and in search of that variety we look to what our neighbour has. We covet our neighbour's ox, especially if it's been slaughtered and is roasting over an open fire. Which obviously makes us sinners.

Time, I think, to examine the ideas behind one of the original commandments. I won't make a habit of this, I promise. Taking the Bible seriously makes my palms itchy. But it's worth getting into, if only briefly.

The full prohibition is not merely on coveting your neighbour's ox, however damn attractive the roasting animal might be, but also their donkey, house, maid, manservant and wife. The humans listed here are classed more as objects than people. At the time the commandments were written, the maid and manservant would have been slaves. And the wife would have been chattel. There is, for example, no mention of wives coveting their neighbours' husbands, not because wives were welcome to do so, but because the original Ten Commandments really didn't give a toss what women thought.

What's important here is the T word: 'thought'. The commandment really is all about what's going on in your head, rather than any action. There are other commandments prohibiting stealing and adultery. But this one is concerned only with thinking about stealing or committing adultery. Or as Jesus is quoted as saying in Matthew 5: 'You have heard that it was said, "Do not commit adultery." But I tell you that anyone who looks at a woman lustfully has already committed adultery with her in his heart.'

Really? Just thinking about doing it is exactly the same as doing it? Oh, my dirty, filthy heart. I believe that was the same logic which was applied by the Stasi in East Germany, and before that by the KGB, to dispatch millions of people to labour camps in the Stalinist Soviet Union. If you were impure of thought, there was a place waiting for you in the salt mines. Bring me my leg irons. The comparison is really not that fanciful, because various biblical scholars have identified this one commandment as an instruction to lead a virtuous life: clear your head of ALL lusts, be satisfied with your lot and dedicate yourself to God. And what was the version of Marxist–Leninist thought as pursued by the Soviet Union if not a religion?

Enough. Talk like this could put you right off your dinner, and that would never do. The point is that wanting what your neighbour has can never be a vice where food is concerned. It is a virtue. It is what spurs us to action. We are meant to roll our eyes at those who sit in restaurants photographing their dinner before slapping those images all over Twitter, Instagram and Facebook. And yes, it can be bloody annoying, especially if they insist upon standing on a chair while doing so. (To be fair, my dinner is also photographed; it's just that when I review I have someone who comes into the restaurant after the fact to photograph it for me.) However, while we roll our eyes it's also worth recognizing that they are part of a digitally accelerated process, that they are merely augmenting our covetousness. If you can remember being delighted by, say, your first Korean chicken wing, or your first proper bowl of ramen made from long-boiled pig bones, or your first Cronut knock-off, then you probably have social media to thank. For almost certainly, without the dissemination of images, enabling a greedy cook somewhere to look at an image and say 'I want that', you wouldn't have got to taste it.

And it's not just about wanting to have what you've seen someone else eating. Sometimes it's about wanting to eat again what someone has cooked for you, or simply about making someone else's recipe your own. Here then are two recipes drawn from my unembarrassed greedy covetousness. Almost all the other recipes in this book started with me, in as much as any recipe begins anywhere. But in a chapter about the importance of other people's food ideas, and of stealing them, these ones have to be someone else's. They come from my hunger to eat more and better and to piggyback on other people's creativity.

JOEL ROBUCHON'S SCALLOPS AND
MORELS UNDER PASTRY

I ate this as part of a dinner cooked for me in the early noughties by both Alain Ducasse and Joel Robuchon, arguably then two of France's greatest high-end chefs, with two or three dozen Michelin stars between them, each taking a course in turn. I cannot recall a single other thing I ate that night because I was transfixed by this one dish. It was, like all the best food items, extremely simple, but fiendishly clever. We were each presented with a medium-sized ramekin, sealed with a dome of golden puff pastry. When we cut in there was the glorious stench of wild mushrooms, for at the bottom was a heap of morels seared in butter and garlic and then covered with a meaty veal jus. Perched on top of that was a single fat king scallop, the size of a baby's fist.

Need I tell you it was delicious, a near-perfect combination of meatiness and sweet shellfish? It was one huge blast of umami. But it was also extraordinarily clever. How did he manage to get the pastry so perfectly burnished and yet not overcook the scallop, for it was just at that point when the protein has set? I lay in bed thinking about this for a week until, like an amateur magician trying to unravel some grand illusion, I finally cracked it.

Of course! At every stage you simply need to make sure everything is fridge cold.

I'll be honest. I have no idea whether this is Robuchon's recipe. I've never checked. But trust me, the result is fabulous, and more than a reminder of the one he served me.

Serves 4

- 50g dried or 175g fresh wild mushrooms (ideally morels, but trompettes are good too)
- 2 tbsp olive oil
- a knob of unsalted butter
- 1 clove of garlic, crushed with the flat blade of a knife, then chopped

sea salt and ground black pepper

100ml veal jus (if you can't get hold of ready-made you'll
need to reduce a litre of veal stock by a factor of ten and
adjust the seasoning. It's a very dull process – trust me
on this. Get ready-made)

4 large king scallops, corals on or off depending on mood
(but why would you remove them?)

1 packet of shop-bought puff pastry

1 egg, beaten

- If using dried mushrooms, soak for half an hour, drain,
  then pat dry.
- Heat the oil in a pan. Wait a minute or two, then add the
  butter.
- Add the mushrooms, and sauté over a medium heat.
  After a couple of minutes add the garlic. Continue
  cooking until the mushrooms start crisping around the
  edges, then season with a little sea salt and black pepper.
- Add the veal jus. Cook over a high heat for a few
  seconds until it's bubbling, scraping at the bottom of the
  pan to pick up rogue bits of garlic and morel.
- Portion the mixture into 4 good-sized ramekins (around
  10cm in diameter), then place in the fridge for at least 2
  hours until completely cold.
- Place a scallop on top of the mixture in each ramekin.
  Season with sea salt. Seal up the mouths of the
  ramekins with the puff pastry. Return to the fridge for
  another hour (or until you are ready to cook and serve).
- Preheat the oven to 200°C/400°F/gas 6. Make sure the
  oven is properly heated before proceeding.
- Glaze the pastry with a little beaten egg. Place in the oven
  for 20 minutes, or until the puff pastry is golden. Serve
  immediately.

CLAYPOT CHICKEN WITH GINGER, FROM
The Vietnamese Market Cookbook BY VAN TRAN
AND ANH VU (SQUARE PEG, 2013)

A confession. I have a wall full of cookbooks but I'm not great at using them. I tend to regard them as an invitation to fail. Which is another way of saying I don't like being told what to do. Generally the ones I gravitate to are those that will supply me with basic methods from which I can build my own dishes, or create versions of others I have eaten in restaurants. But with the Asian repertoire you really can't make it up, and *The Vietnamese Market Cookbook* is a fabulous way into a particularly nuanced culinary tradition, influenced as much by its colonial past as its geographical position.

This is the recipe I cook from it most often, though adapted a little. I am grateful to the authors for granting me permission to use it. They say 300g of chicken will serve four. Not in my house it won't, and certainly not when they've tasted this. So I've scaled it up. Some of the volumes look shocking. They are correct. It is quite simply the most outrageous marinade you will ever make. Put it this way: you'll want to buy a jar of ready-crushed garlic and another of ground black pepper

Serves 4

1kg chicken thighs, skin on, bone in
3 tbsp vegetable oil
1 tbsp crushed garlic
150g fresh ginger, peeled and thinly sliced
4 tbsp water

For the marinade

3 tbsp crushed garlic
3 tbsp chopped shallots
3 tbsp vegetable oil

4 tbsp sugar
9 tbsp fish sauce
2 tbsp ground black pepper
1 tsp sea salt
1 tsp garlic powder

- In a bowl, combine the marinade ingredients with the chicken thighs. Mix, then cover and leave in the fridge for an hour.
- In a heavy-bottomed pan, heat the vegetable oil with the crushed garlic and the ginger and toss until fragrant (a couple of minutes at most).
- Pour in the chicken and all of the marinade and heat in the oil for a minute or two. Add the water. Make sure the thighs are skin-side down. Half cover with a lid and cook over a low heat for 45 minutes.
- The original recipe seems to call for the chicken to be served at this point. I disagree because I don't like undercooked chicken skin. It's time to reduce the liquor down and to caramelize the chicken. Turn the heat up and stand over it, scraping at the bottom. Beware: there's so much sugar in there it can burn, so keep watch. Keep it moving. Get the pieces of chicken in contact with the bottom of the pan, so that the skin colours up.
- When the chicken is sticky, and the sauce cooked out to solid, serve with all the fabulous gunk from the bottom of the pan.
- It happens to be brilliant cold the next day.

4.

Thou shalt cook – sometimes

This one looks inarguable, doesn't it? Of course thou shalt bloody cook. Only ignorant numpties with palates blunted by a military-scale assault of salt and sugar courtesy of an overdose of festering, Technicolor takeaways don't bother cooking their food from scratch. Now just give us a couple of your recipes and move on to the next commandment.

Except it's not quite that simple.

Throughout human history technological developments have enabled the repeated migration of mundane tasks from the many to the few so that, free from unnecessary drudgery, we can get on with doing something altogether more interesting. In 1870, for example, between 70 per cent and 80 per cent of the American population were engaged in agriculture. That many people were needed simply to get the job done and keep the population fed. A lot of them grew food just for themselves and their families. Thankfully, mechanization and then automation changed all that, because it was brutally hard work. By 2008, fewer than 2 per cent of Americans were producing food for the rest. Britain, a smaller and more crowded country, saw a similar decline, albeit from a lower base. At the 1841 census, 22 per cent of the UK population were farmers. Now it's less than 1 per cent. The only people who grow their own food these days are those who have made a lifestyle choice to do so; the ones who enjoy banging on about how much better their lettuce tastes than the stuff you buy at the supermarket, and the fact that the chickens they keep for eggs have characters as distinct as Labradors. (They don't.)

A couple of centuries ago the vast majority of the population made their own clothes. Today, it is a job for eccentric hobbyists, who don't mind going out looking like they were dressed by a blind person while standing in a wind tunnel. The rest of us don't do this, because we know others can make our clothes or grow our food for us both more quickly and more cheaply – if you calculate in the cost of your own labour accurately. In an age where sustainability matters, mass production also has a smaller carbon footprint than food and clothes produced by the amateur end-user. There is a carbon benefit in large scale.

So why can't the same apply to finished dishes? Isn't there a logic to allowing corporations to do all the hard graft of chopping and frying and stirring for you? It's a point made by the American food historian Rachel Laudan in her groundbreaking essay 'A Plea for Culinary Modernism', first published in *Gastronomica* in February 2001. Naming the self-appointed protectors of our culinary traditions – the 'artisanal', local, seasonal mob – 'culinary luddites', she points out that throughout human history we have advanced by finding ways to make edible those foods which in their natural state would be deeply unpalatable. As she says, 'to make food tasty, safe, digestible and healthy our forebears bred, ground, soaked, leached, curdled, fermented and cooked naturally occurring plants and animals until they were literally beaten into submission'. In other words they processed them. What's more, pre-prepared foods have been a feature of city life for centuries, due to restricted access to cooking apparatus and the cost of manufacture in the home. In twelfth-century Baghdad 'the townspeople bought ready-cooked meats, salt fish, bread and a broth of dried chick peas', Laudan writes. The Mexicans have been visiting takeaway taco stands for centuries, while in Japan they have been buying fish stews outside the home for just as long.

Deep-frying, a focus of modern angst, has long been performed outside of the domestic setting, not least because it's bloody dangerous. And developments in food technology like this have been hugely important for a population trying to scrape by. 'No amount of nostalgia for the pastoral foods of the distant past,' Laudan writes, 'can wish away the fact that our ancestors lived mean, short lives constantly afflicted with diseases, many of which can be directly attributed to what they did and did not eat.' Laudan concludes by pointing out that were the culinary clock turned backwards, women would be stuck in the kitchen every hour of the day, and many people would be starving.

It's an assertion echoed by the writer Michael Pollen in his 2013 book, *Cooked*: 'The outsourcing of much of the work of cooking to corporations has relieved women of what has traditionally been the exclusive responsibility for feeding the family, making it easier for them to work outside the home and have careers.' He makes the point seriously (in a book which, to be fair, goes on to argue exactly the opposite), but it has not only been made by him. As Pollen states, in the 1970s Kentucky Fried Chicken advertised their product in the US by putting the words 'Women's Liberation' above a picture of a bucket of their fried chicken. Feed the family this, dear old KFC was saying, and you can get on with doing something far more interesting and fulfilling.

But it's not just about the hard labour involved in getting food on the table. It's about the food itself. In December 2014 a paper in the *Journal of Preventative Medicine* looked at the health of 2,000 American women between the ages of forty-two and fifty-two. It found that the odds of metabolic syndrome – high glucose levels, low levels of 'good' cholesterol, hypertension, and so on – increased not just with age but especially among those who spent more time preparing meals. It seemed they didn't just cook more. They ate too much of their own output as well.

If studies of the nutritional value of the recipes written by high-profile chefs are anything to go by, this negative impact isn't entirely surprising. A paper published in the journal *Food and Public Health* in April 2013 looked at 904 recipes from twenty-six

UK-based celebrity chefs (based on the top 100 bestselling cookbooks of 2009 and those individuals featured as celebrity chefs on the Food Channel's website). Around 87 per cent of those recipes 'fell substantially short of the UK government's healthy eating recommendations'. According to Dr Ricardo Costa, senior lecturer and researcher in dietetics at Coventry University, 'If people regularly use the recipes found in these cookbooks it could be that celebrity chefs are exacerbating public health and nutrition issues in the UK.'

A 2012 study from Newcastle University, which compared recipes with ready meals, found something similar. Jamie Oliver had a recipe for a meatball sandwich with pickled cabbage and chopped salad which was 1,000 calories per serving. A Nigella Lawson recipe for beer-braised pork knuckle with caraway, garlic, apples and potatoes was 1,340 calories per serving. Hugh Fearnley-Whittingstall had a recipe for a leek and cheese tart that contained a whacking 217g of saturated fat, when Britain's National Health Service recommends no more than 30g a day for an adult male. By comparison the most calorific supermarket ready meal the researchers could find, a chicken tikka masala with pilau rice from Tesco, had 870 calories.

So is there really no evidence that cooking your own food is better for you? Yes, there is some, though it's hardly a slam dunk. A paper from the Johns Hopkins Bloomberg School of Public Health in Baltimore, published in November 2014, did indeed find a health benefit to cooking at home, but the size of that benefit is questionable. Almost half the sample studied said they cooked dinner from scratch six or seven days a week, and consumed 2,164 calories a day while doing so. Just 8 per cent cooked dinner once or less a week, and consumed 2,301 calories a day. That's a difference of less than 6 per cent, and in any case deals only with the extremes. We can safely assume that the difference between those cooking, say, three times a week and those cooking six times a week would have been even smaller. Furthermore, the study was based on a self-reporting sample, which is notoriously unreliable, especially where what people are really shoving in their mouths is concerned. For what it's worth, and entirely anecdotally, in my experience it's the compulsive home cooks who are the greediest. Their desire to cook is driven less by an imperative to be healthy but because they love their food – both the process involved in producing it and the reward of eating it at the end.

Instinctively we want to believe that cooking food from scratch is healthier for us than the alternative, and of course it can be. It can mean you are in complete control of the levels of fat, sugar and salt in your food. The distance between raw ingredients and the finished dish is generally shorter than something that has gone through the mass retail system, so presumably it is nutritionally better (though if you're eating a balanced diet you won't be suffering from scurvy or rickets, whatever route your ingredients took to get to the table). And just because a recipe looks calorific doesn't mean those following it are eating unhealthily. As the NHS Choices website said, in response to the report finding high calorie values in celebrity chef's recipes, 'We cannot draw reliable conclusions on the effects of these findings because, for example, we don't know if these recipes are cooked and eaten frequently.'

Instinct, intuition and even best practice might give us a model whereby cooking food from scratch could be better for you. But none of that is the same thing as hard evidence, and the hard evidence on the virtues of cooking your food yourself rather than getting someone else to do so is nowhere near as conclusive as some might wish. Sure, it can be. But it's not in any way guaranteed.

Plus, we need to give ourselves a break. We lead busy lives. For example, who the hell has the time to make their own puff pastry, when you can get a more than adequate version from the shop? I can't for the life of me imagine why anyone makes their own tomato ketchup or mayonnaise, or why you would bother to soak beans from dried when the canned variety do the job brilliantly. And you know what: getting a takeaway or a ready meal every now and then is not the end of the world. Sometimes time is short. Sometimes there really are more important things in this world than cooking.

Which means that I have to work much harder to come up with a robust argument for why we should cook at all, and here it is: cooking is fun.

That's fun in the very broadest sense of the word. Cooking makes you feel better about yourself. It gives you skills. It bends the world to your will. Human beings used to be makers. We used to make our own tools and clothes. We used to build our own houses and furniture, and toys for the kids. We whittled sticks and dug holes and planted fruit trees and crops. We did all these things because we had to.

Unless it happens to be your job, unless you are paid by others to do so on their behalf, we don't do any of that any more, hobbyists aside. And like those who make their own clothes, the hobbyists are defined by the eccentricity of what they do. Making pots in your spare time, or having an interest in carpentry or needlepoint, is remarkable precisely because the rest of us make nothing.

Apart from dinner. That, we all can make.

The problem is it's *not* easy. We're told to think otherwise, of course. The cookbook section of www.amazon.co.uk has over 27,000 books with the word 'easy' in the title. It's all *Eating Well Made Easy* and *River Cottage Light and Easy* and *Baking Made Easy*. There are over 18,000 books with the word 'quick' in the title, and 6,000 deploying the word 'simple'. There are only eleven with the word 'complicated' on the front, but they use it merely to describe how the book is the antidote to such a concept, as in *Complicated Living Doesn't Need Complicated Food*.

Cooking takes time and practice and effort. It is not one discipline, but many. It's about the impact of hot water on meat and vegetables, and the entirely different impact of dry heat on those ingredients, or heat transmitted through various fats. It's about emulsions, and what happens to the protein in eggs when you beat them, or gluten in flour when you use it to make a dough. It's a lifetime's learning, which will never be completed, but which joyously has a purpose, for we all need to eat.

Compared to the chefs I write about I would class myself as a moderately competent cook, but it was not always so. For many years I was awful. I arrived at Leeds University in the mid 1980s thinking that pouring a can of Campbell's cream of mushroom soup over two pieces of chicken and putting that in the oven was an entirely reasonable thing to do. It wasn't. It should have been classed as bad manners. I bought the wrong cut of beef, assuming it to be entirely serviceable as steak, without knowing I couldn't afford the right cut. Incinerating it under a scorching grill didn't help any. In my third year my parents came to visit me, and I made them something terrifying involving beef in red wine from which the alcohol had not been entirely expunged. I can still recall the acrid, sour liquor; the way it tasted of overarching ambition, ignorance and failure. It would help if I could blame those same parents for sending me off into the world without the necessary skills, but they were not guilty as charged, because they did try. There is a photograph of me, aged about nine, in the family kitchen, wearing an apron and using a knife to scrape the last of the fat – possibly margarine: it was the 1970s – from a container. I would have been baking banana bread, because that was what I always baked. I imagine my mother was proud of me the first time I did it, and dreamed of a future full of varied cakes made by her youngest child. I imagine she was somewhat weary on the ninth occasion that it turned out to be banana bread.

As a teenager, home alone, I did truly awful things to a well-seasoned wok using Chinese ingredients that I hoped would help me replicate the salty aromatic dishes we ate as a family each Christmas in the steamy Cantonese places along London's

Queensway near Hyde Park. Because that's how Jews have always celebrated the birth of the baby Jesus. Really. It's true. Eating Chinese food at Christmas is a mitzvah for non-observant, non-religious Jews. So I knew what the food tasted like. I just couldn't make it.

Things got better. In my early twenties my then girlfriend (now wife) asked for cookbooks for her birthday, but I was the one who started using them. I learned how to make a stuffing for turkey involving Parma ham and chestnuts, marjoram and Marsala wine. I came up with better ways to use mushrooms in chicken casseroles, stole a recipe from my sister for a double rack of lamb filled with breadcrumbs, basil, olives and sun-dried tomatoes, and used instructions for crumbly pastry from a book published by *Reader's Digest*, which I still refer to occasionally, to make my own onion tart (see the recipe on page 51). I discovered that if I knew some basics, I could start to work out how dishes eaten in restaurants were made, even without the recipe.

We all know and understand the serious, occasionally pious reasons underlying the imperative to learn to cook. If you're skint it's easier to eat well, because you can transform the cheapest of ingredients through the application of your free labour. You learn about nutrition by putting the ingredients together yourself, which has to be a good thing, and you free yourself from the aesthetic sensibilities of corporations offering you their limited choices, or choices overinfluenced by the vagaries and bad taste of fashion.

I know all of this, and agree with it. But really what I love about cooking is its functionality. Very few of us make our livings from finite tasks. A lot of modern work is open-ended, with projects lasting days, weeks or even years at a time. One process bleeds into another. Another job begins before the last has finished. We head towards finishing lines that seem to move before we've got there. Our children refuse to do as we say; our orphaned socks refuse to find their pair. We think of ourselves as powerful, but most of the time, faced by the knotty complexities of life, we are impotent. We are twigs borne along on life's currents.

And then there's cooking, which is completely self-contained. I enter the kitchen, choose my ingredients and make them do as I say. I make a huge great steaming mess, but know that from this chaos will eventually come a certain order. (For what it's worth, I do not own a dishwasher, for I enjoy the process of washing up. I like its rhythm, the way it is purely a means to an end. For those staring aghast at the page, you should know I am in a minority of one on this in my family, and the kitchen is soon to get a dishwasher.) What's more, out of the chaos that you create and then rectify comes something else: dinner. The effort has purpose. You have proved that you can look after yourself.

It is a lesson we are trying to communicate to our kids. My wife, Pat, and our youngest, Dan, twelve years old at the time of writing, have a baking blog (dansamazingbreadfactory). It began with him proposing ideas. Would it be possible to make chocolate bread? Or peanut butter bread? Or bread flavoured with his favourite snack of salami, cheese and crackers? (Answer: yes, it would – a cheese roll, flavoured with finely chopped chorizo and topped with crumbled and then baked crackers.) Coming up with the ideas has always been fun, but more important than that is the process. Dan likes to knead bread. He's good at it, knows how to throw and push. Sure, he performs the task knowing where it will end, which is to say with bread. But when he is hands-deep in the dough itself, he is in the present. Merely watching him do that explains to me why we should all cook sometimes.

And so the first of these two recipes – for cottage pie buns – is Dan's idea, developed into a recipe by my other half, Pat. Dan adores cottage pie, and who can blame him. The question was, how could you get the two elements – the long-cooked mince below, the mash on top – into a bread product? Pat's solution was the potato-based dough used here. I won't lie: not every one of their bread-factory products has worked for me. I wasn't a huge fan of their 'indeterminate green soup bread' – a roll flavoured with soup made from all the vegetables left in the chiller drawer of the fridge at the end of the week, as a way to avoid waste. It had a back taste of damp field in November. But these buns are fabulous. They're not simple or quick to make, but then, as I've already said, cooking isn't always. Think of them as a Yorkshire version of the Chinese char siu bun, one bite revealing the cavity inside stuffed with sticky meatiness.

If you want a three-word answer to the question 'Why cook?', the words 'cottage pie buns' will do brilliantly.

COTTAGE PIE BUNS

You can use lamb mince for these instead, but then, of course, they would be shepherd's pie buns.

Makes 14 buns (enough for 7 greedy people)

For the buns

600g Maris Piper potatoes
2 tsp dried yeast
2 tsp caster sugar
2 tbsp olive oil, plus extra to grease
1 tbsp fine sea salt
600g strong white flour
1 egg, beaten

For the cottage pie filling

500g beef mince
500g pork mince
olive oil for frying
1 large onion, diced
2 medium-sized carrots, diced
2 sticks of celery, diced
1 tbsp tomato puree
1 tsp mixed dried herbs
sea salt and ground black pepper
1 tsp honey
750ml beef or chicken stock from cubes

- Start by making the cottage pie filling. In a bowl, mix the beef and pork mince by hand.
- Heat the olive oil in a large casserole pot. Gently fry the onion, carrots and celery until softened. Add the mince, and brown.

- Add the tomato puree, herbs and a little salt and black pepper to season, and mix well.
- Dissolve the honey into the stock, then pour over the meat. Bring to the boil, then turn down the heat so the mixture is only just bubbling. Leave to bubble for at least 2 hours. If it appears to be cooking dry, add a little more stock. At the end it should be thick and glossy, without any liquid. Allow to cool.
- Next make the buns. Peel the potatoes, chop into even chunks and cook in a pan of boiling salted water until tender but not falling apart. Drain in a colander, then return to the pan and toss over a very low heat for a couple of minutes until any excess liquid has evaporated.
- Pour 75ml of cool water into a large bowl and sprinkle in the yeast. Stir in the sugar and leave in a warm place for about 10 minutes until a light foam appears.
- Mash the potatoes with the 2 tablespoons of olive oil until smooth, then stir into the yeast mixture with the salt. Mix well with a wooden spoon and gradually add the flour a few tablespoons at a time, stirring well. When the dough becomes too stiff to stir, turn it out on to a work surface and knead any remaining flour into it. Knead for 10 minutes until soft. Do not add any more water.
- Put in a lightly oiled bowl. Cover with cling film and leave to rise in a warm place for 2 hours.
- Divide the risen dough into 14 equal pieces. Roll each into a ball and then flatten into a disc. Put a couple of tablespoons of the cottage pie mixture into the middle of each disc, press it down gently, then bring the edges of the disc in to cover. Massage gently to form a round bun.
- Prove the buns for an hour on a lightly greased baking

sheet, inside a plastic bag, in a warm place. Meanwhile, preheat the oven to 200°C/400°F/gas 6. Once the buns have risen, glaze with the egg and bake for 25 minutes.

- Allow to cool for 20 minutes, then serve, still warm.

MY ONION TART

I'm sure this is not particularly different from anybody else's. It just happens to be the way I make it. I use pâte brisée, a French shortcrust pastry, because it produces a thinner, crisper shell, but you could just as easily use shop-bought shortcrust, or if you really fancy, just put the onion mixture on a big square of shop-bought puff pastry. Just make sure to score a line around each side an inch or so in from the edge, and glaze generously with egg wash to get a nicely risen frame.

For the tart shell

200g flour, plus extra to dust
100g cold unsalted butter, cut into pieces
1 egg yolk
½ tsp sea salt
45ml water

For the filling

2 tbsp olive oil
3 medium-sized onions, of any colour (a mixture of white and red if you like). sliced into rings
50g unsalted butter
1 tbsp balsamic vinegar
sea salt and ground black pepper
2 eggs
50g fresh Parmesan, grated

- First make the pastry. Sift the flour on to a work surface, making a well in the middle for the butter, egg yolk, sea salt and water. Use your fingertips to gradually bring all the ingredients together, including the flour from the edges. Work it until you get coarse crumbs.
- Bring everything together into a ball, lightly flour the work surface and knead with the heel of your hand. It will take a couple of minutes for the dough to become putty-like. Roll into a ball, cover with cling film and chill in the fridge for 30 minutes.
- Flour the surface again, and gently begin to roll out. Make sure to lift the dough every three or four rolls so it doesn't stick. Add a dusting of flour to keep it moving. You want a disc with a 30cm diameter.
- Having read this far, you may have decided to buy shortcrust pastry. I won't judge you.
- Preheat the oven to 220°C/425°F/gas 7.
- Grease a 25cm tart tin, and line it with the pastry by rolling it round a rolling pin so it can be gently unrolled over the tin. Press into the edges with your thumb. Prick the bottom with a fork (to prevent air bubbles forming), then blind bake, by lining with greaseproof paper and weighing it down with dried beans or, if you have them, ceramic baking beans.
- Bake for 10 minutes, then turn the oven down to 190°C/375°F/gas 5 and cook for a further 5 minutes. Remove from the oven, take out the beans and grease-proof paper and allow to cool before gently removing the shell from the tin. Place straight on to the oven rack you will be cooking it on once filled.
- To make the filling, gently heat the oil in a high-sided frying pan and add the onions. They will look like an enormous heap, but they will cook down. Sauté on a low heat for 5 minutes, moving them around

occasionally so those at the top get time at the bottom.

- Sprinkle the butter in pieces around the pan, and continue cooking for 20 to 30 minutes until you have a tangle of translucent onions.
- Turn up the heat to high and add the balsamic vinegar. Mix it well with the onions and fry for 2 or 3 minutes so some start to catch and crisp. Season with sea salt and black pepper.
- Allow to cool for at least 10 minutes, or more if convenient. (You can get both the onions and the tart shell to this point a couple of hours ahead of when you need them.)
- Turn the oven back up to 200°C / 400°F / gas 6.
- Spread the onion mixture around the inside of the tart shell. Beat the eggs with a fork, then mix in the grated Parmesan. Pour the egg / Parmesan mixture over the onions, moving it all around to spread evenly.
- Bake for 10 to 15 minutes, or until the pastry is golden brown and the egg has set. Allow to cool for 5 minutes or so, then serve.

5

Thou shalt not cut off the fat

A chilly November lunchtime and I am at home in the warm, preparing to indulge in a little risky personal behaviour. I am excited by the prospect of taking my life in my hands. I like living on the edge. In front of me is a tightly wrapped paper package, stamped with the logo of my local butcher's. I slide a knife through the tape that's keeping the paper in place, and half expect warning sirens to go off as I fold it back to reveal the treasure within: a 200g piece of Welsh-reared prime Wagyu steak. At £100 a kilo it's one of the most expensive pieces of beef available in Britain, or anywhere else for that matter. The cult of Wagyu began in Japan, where it's known generally as Kobe beef, after the capital city of Hyōgo Prefecture in which, most famously, this breed is raised.

The risk here is presented less by the red meat – though obviously that does raise issues – than by its fat content. Wagyu is prized for its fat marbling. Legend has it that in Kobe all the animals were once fed beer and massaged to increase that marbling (though the practice is now dying out). All beef has a thick ribbon of gloriously saturated amber fat around the edge of each individual muscle, with a little, depending on breed, inside the muscle. With Wagyu, the whole point is the intramuscular fat, which threads through it to such a degree that the meat looks veal pink rather than red when viewed from a distance. Close up there is a lacy, almost fragile quality to the raw flesh. And of course, being determined to do this properly, I have chosen a rib-eye, one of the fattiest cuts of an already fatty animal. There are thick, hard jewels of solid fat right in the middle of the steak.

I find this thrilling, because I love fat. I can't quite imagine why some people don't. I love the crunch and the drip and the richness; the way it coats the mouth. There is nothing more depressing to me at the table than watching someone cut the crisped and golden curve of fat off the back of a lamb chop, discard the crackling from pork, nudge the crunchy blistered chicken skin to one side of the plate. I want to lean across the table, sink the tines of my fork into the softest part of their hand and shout, 'Stop! Don't you know that fat is where the flavour is?'

Because it is.

But I don't do this, because I am too much of a gentleman. Instead I go my own way, which is exactly what I am doing this morning, here in my kitchen. The Wagyu steak has been allowed to come up to room temperature. I put a dry frying pan on a high heat for ten minutes, until it is smoking, then rub the meat with a light gloss of olive oil and season generously with sea salt and ground black pepper. Now all it needs is ninety seconds on each side in the pan, and a ten-minute rest on a warm plate. I stand over it as the seared muscle, now bronzed to the colour of copper coins, gently begins to relax. I use a sharp knife to slice it into 1cm-thick pieces. I can see that it's still a baby's bottom pink at the heart of each slice. I sigh with relief. I have done this extraordinarily expensive piece of meat justice. It is not overcooked.

I eat the Wagyu, still standing there by the stove, with my fingers, the juices dribbling down them. The meat has a rich minerality, an uncommon earthiness. The charred outside is, of course, an umami bomb, the very definition of savoury; if it's not stating the bloody obvious, which it is, there is a pronounced meatiness. But there's something else too: a rich but gentle lubrication, a pleasing slipperiness full of deeper, life-affirming tones. It's the fat.

God, but I love fat.

In 1980 the US government did its very best to stop this sort of sordid, filthy behaviour. They finally issued official advice warning against a diet high in saturated fats, of the sort found in beef and various other meat products, as well as in full-fat milk and dairy in general. Saturated fats are so called because their chemical formula is filled up – saturated – with hydrogen atoms; unsaturated fats have fewer bonds to hydrogen atoms. The health advice was clear: a diet heavy in these saturated fats was a cause of heart disease. Unsaturated fats of the sort found in vegetable oils were apparently better for you.

The decision to issue this dietary advice was understandable given the incidence of heart disease; if anything the authorities had been slow to act. By the late 1950s, heart disease had increased to such a degree in the US that it had become the country's number one killer. In 1900 it accounted for 137 deaths per 100,000 people. By 1960 it was 369 deaths per 100,000. In 1955 even President Eisenhower, arguably the most medically supervised individual in the country, had suffered a heart attack.

A compelling explanation for this pandemic was needed. It was provided by Dr Ancel Benjamin Keys of the University of Minnesota. He oversaw the post-war Seven Countries Study, which looked at 13,000 men in the US, Japan and Europe. He found that heart disease was caused not by ageing, as had long been believed, but by diet. What's more, he said, it was the countries with the lowest levels of saturated fat in the diet which had the lowest levels of heart disease.

The instruction to remove fat, and especially saturated fat, from the diet spread around the world, and in January 1961 took Dr Keys to the very cover of *Time* magazine. He was the doctor who had diagnosed the disease of modern life. Quickly, it became orthodoxy. Our supermarket aisles reflected the doctrine of low fat: low-fat butter substitutes and yoghurts, low-fat cakes and puddings and breads and salad dressings. Fat was the enemy, and everybody knew the best defence. If you have ever wondered why we all used to drink full-fat milk and then switched to skimmed or semi-skimmed, the answer is Dr Ancel Benjamin Keys.

For me the idea that fatness came from fat made sense. I have always both loved fat and been fat. I like to joke that I have a metabolism engineered for a brutal winter on the Russian Steppes when the Cossacks are coming. Like all the best jokes, it is laced with a certain truth. Us Eastern European Jews, or at least my family's bit of them, have often tended to store excess energy around our hips and thighs and belly. Now, living a comfortable life in the inner London suburbs, I have no one to run away from. The fat I so love to eat may safely accumulate. I could understand why the American government had issued its health advice back in 1980, not that I was brilliant at following it.

Except, if I'd bothered to look, I would have noticed that something curious happened the moment that advice was issued. From 1980 onwards, rates of obesity in the US (and, later, elsewhere) started climbing, and dramatically. By 2015 they had more than doubled in the US to 35 per cent of the population, with 69 per cent defined as either overweight or obese. As the years passed, various researchers would begin to finger the culprit: the nutritional advice itself. Faced by an imperative to reduce all that terrible fat, food manufacturers started upping the levels of sugars – refined carbohydrates – in their products, to make them more palatable. The problem is that these sugars break down to become glucose, which in turn causes the release of insulin. That encourages weight gain, and creates risk factors for Type 2 diabetes (the form generally caused by lifestyle and diet rather than acquired at birth), which, alongside weight gain in general, is related to heart disease. In the history of unintended consequences, this one was a cracker: pulling out the so-called dangerous fats appeared to have unleashed an even more dangerous tidal wave of sugars.

Soon questions were being asked about the methodology of the great Dr Keys, slayer of saturated fats. For example, it turned out that his Seven Countries Study had been rather selective. He had excluded countries like France, where they have never met an animal fat they didn't like, and Switzerland, a country where the national dish, cheese fondue, is so rich it's easy to imagine American health officials classing it alongside fags as a killer. (See the recipe below.) And yet, despite eating these diets high in saturated fats, neither France nor Switzerland had reported a high incidence of heart disease.

There were also issues around Dr Keys's most important example of a population where a low-saturated-fat diet appeared to equal a low incidence of heart disease. It was based on a sample of peasant farmers on the Greek island of Crete in the years immediately following the Second World War, when the diet was exceptionally meagre and therefore not typical. It didn't help that they were studied partly during Lent, when, for religious reasons, those farmers had sworn off meat and dairy. And while Keys had initially started out with a sample of 655 men, problems with the survey meant he had to rely on findings from just a few dozen. It took until 2002 for these problems to be raised, but by then the anti-fat dogma was entrenched.

Alongside the questioning of the great Dr Keys came a bunch of meta-studies – the bringing together of findings from many other studies of the same subject – which examined the charge sheet against saturated fat. The problem, it seems, is that too many of the studies which fingered those fats as the villain failed to look at the rest of the subjects' diet and lifestyle. They didn't check to see how much carbohydrate might also be in that diet, or whether they were smokers, a clear marker for heart disease. The conclusive proof that saturated fats cause heart disease simply didn't seem to be there.

Slowly but surely, scientists and campaigners have rallied to their defence. The American journalist Nina Teicholz, author of *The Big Fat Surprise: Why Butter, Meat and Cheese Belong in a Healthy Diet*, has argued that saturated fats were wrongly demonized as a result of 'personal ambition, bad science, politics and bias'. Dr Keys simply found a way to make his name and he wasn't about to let it go.

Teicholz also points out that the move from saturated fats led to the over-consumption of vegetable fats and the greater use of 'trans-fats' – artificially hydrogenated vegetable oils, which melt at a higher temperature than standard vegetable oils. Because they stay solid at higher temperatures, industrial food processors found them easier to work with. These were later discovered to be exceptionally dangerous to human health, raising levels of 'bad' cholesterol and furring arteries. In June 2015 the US Food and Drink Administration announced that trans-fats would have to be removed from all foodstuffs over the following three years, where possible. (A small number of foodstuffs have small amounts of naturally occurring trans-fats.)

However, nearly two years earlier, in September 2013, news from Sweden had arrived that those preaching the gospel of fat had long been waiting for: the Swedish Council on Health Technology Assessment issued advice based on a survey of 16,000 obesity studies. They found that a low-carb diet could lead to greater weight loss in obese individuals than a low-fat diet could; that a high intake of full-fat dairy products could lead to weight loss in obese children and adults; and that a Mediterranean diet – high in olive oil and nuts – could lead to lower levels of heart disease than a diet low in fats. Then, in March 2014, the journal *Annals of Internal Medicine* published a big report which included the news that 'saturated fat does not cause heart disease'.

Hurrah! Smear me in lard and call me Dorothy. My love of fat was not to blame for the shape in which I had found myself. The good times were back.

Or perhaps not. In all the excitement, certain journalists (including, *cough*, this one) mistook the Swedish Council on Health Technology Assessment for the Swedish government itself. We insisted that Sweden was the first Western government to abandon the low-fat orthodoxy. Except they were not the government at all, just an advisory body, and Sweden's health officials were not about to start proposing low-carb diets for the entire population.

That said, there is no doubt that the idea of saturated animal fats as the sole villain of the piece has been firmly discredited. Many meta-studies find no evidence that they are the ones to blame. A number have found some evidence of an impact on heart disease, but have not been able to conclude whether it was directly life-threatening. The confusion is partly down to the way the mass media reports science. Journalists assume that scientists are bringers of truth; if you have a PhD, a reporter will take what you say as fact, not least because you've spent longer in education than they could bring themselves to. In reality, scientists merely bring data, the analysis of which is little more than a stepping stone towards some wider understanding of how the world might work. What's more, both that data and its analysis are easily confused and muddied by failures of sample size, collection, or because the person doing the analysing has an axe to grind.

Increasingly it seems that when it comes to the relationship between what we eat and our health, what matters is not what one person in a white coat says compared to what another person in a white coat says. It's about the entirety of our diet and how we calculate risk.

A closely related example: in October 2015 the World Health Organization announced that bacon, sausages and processed meats in general were now to be classified as a Group 1 carcinogen, alongside tobacco, asbestos and arsenic, because of a causal link with bowel cancer. That was enough to ruin anybody's Monday.

Bacon, fabulous bacon, with its gloriously brittle meat and crisped fat, its hit of salt and sweet; the one ingredient that wavering vegetarians admit can pull them from the path of righteousness; the one foodstuff the application of which makes every single dish ever invented so much better: this was now to be regarded as a killer? Like fags? Certainly that's what a lot of headlines suggested. How could that be?

Obviously, faced by news like this, I did the only sensible thing. I made myself a proper bacon sandwich – smoked streaky, fried until crisp, a crusty roll, a smear of ketchup – and settled down to study the numbers. Firstly, it turns out that while a Group 1 rating means a substance is carcinogenic to humans, it doesn't explain exactly how carcinogenic. Some substances will send you straight to the cancer clinic and invite you to write farewell notes to your loved ones. Others will impact upon you very little. The rating doesn't make a distinction; all it says is that a link has been made. Secondly, what matters is risk. The analysis announced that eating a 50g portion of processed meat a day leads to an 18 per cent increase in the risk of getting bowel cancer, which sounds deeply worrying.

But that's an 18 per cent increase on the already pre-existing risk of getting bowel cancer. In the UK the lifetime risk of bowel cancer is 5 per cent, which means that eating a 50g portion a day increases your risk by 18 per cent of 5 per cent, or less than 1 per cent. That takes it to just under 6 per cent. (By comparison, smoking just a few cigarettes a day increases a woman's risk of getting lung cancer by 400 per cent.)

But of course these are general figures, based on a broad brushstroke analysis of an entire population. As the *Washington Post* pointed out at the time, this does not account for those people who are genetically immune to certain cancers, as some lucky people are. But there's something else. It also doesn't account for your wider lifestyle choices, in the same way that too many of the flawed saturated-fat studies didn't.

So yes, I eat bacon and, more to the point, I eat saturated fats. And I am overweight – less overweight than I once was, but overweight all the same. However, there are a whole bunch of other risk factors that have to be considered on a case-by-case basis. For example, I haven't smoked with any meaningful enthusiasm for well over twenty years, or at all in the past five years. I drink alcohol, but not to excess. I eat a lot of fruit and vegetables, avoid bread in particular and unrefined carbs in general and, believe it or not, have a pronounced gym habit. Because I'm terrified of how I look on camera when I'm doing TV work, I run off to the gym at least four times a week and often more. I wear a headband to keep my hair in place. Telling you about the hairband has nothing to do with explaining risk factors. I'm just getting it out there now in case you ever come across me in a gym and find the sight shocking. Don't judge me.

Your risk of dying early or not isn't based around your choices between a bunch of Alice in Wonderland-type ingredients marked 'Eat Me' or 'Don't Eat Me'. While it might be easier if the world worked like that, it doesn't. It is the sum of your entire lifestyle. If you smoke twenty fags a day, drink a bottle of vodka a night, adore grim, sugar-sodden white bread with the consistency of marshmallow and spend most of your time sprawled on the sofa, then no, you might not want to go big on the saturated fats.

But that's fine. That's terrific. All the more meat and dairy for me then.

A liking for fat is a matter of taste. Or to put it another way, people with good taste like it. This may not simply be a sweeping value judgement (though it's certainly that). Increasingly it appears to be a physiological truth. A growing body of evidence is leading researchers towards the conclusion that fat is the sixth distinct taste, alongside sweet, salt, bitter, sour and umami. Studies from both Deakin University in Australia and Purdue University, Indiana, in the US, published in 2015, identified fats as having a clear and distinct taste, and theorized that just as with the others, there would be receptors on the tongue designed to recognize those fats and communicate their presence to the brain. The Purdue study went so far as to give this taste a name: *oleogustus*, from the Latin *oleum* for oil and *gustus* for taste. It would be a huge discovery if proven, akin to the announcement of another primary colour. Given how easily we distinguish in our mouths between high-fat products and their counterfeit low-fat versions, the existence of oleogustus would make sense.

What role oleogustus might have in our diets is less certain. That said, it might explain why, just as there are those who don't like sweet things because they don't have the taste receptors to do so, there are others who don't like fat. They simply don't have the physical equipment to enjoy it. Those poor, poor people. It is striking to me that the people I regard as fellow travellers – the ones who also like eating with their hands; who, like me, run towards offal rather than away from it and who don't have issues with texture; the ones who don't moan about hair and nipples on pork scratchings but ask for another bag; the greedy people – are the ones who also recognize the importance of fat to the joy and pleasure of food.

If you want proof of fat's importance, try cooking pork fillet (or pork tenderloin as it's sometimes known). Like beef fillet, the muscle is used for posture rather than motion and, not being heavily worked, tends to be less tough than others. Chefs like it, especially in the sort of television cooking shows I sometimes judge, because it's easy to cook precisely and it slices up tidily, which makes it obliging when it comes to making plates look pretty. It is also, like beef fillet, almost fat-free. And as a result it tastes of next to nothing. At best it is a lump of vaguely salty protein. Frankly, I've chewed on more interesting pillows. This is because flavour molecules dissolve in fat, and without any, the mechanism by which you would experience the intense pigginess just isn't there. A piece of pig without any flavour is a terrible waste of a noble animal.

Unless of course you disagree with me, and regard pork fillet as the greatest cut of meat known to humanity. In which case don't bother with the recipes below. There is nothing for you to enjoy there at all. Skip to the next commandment.

SWISS CHEESE FONDUE

My late mother-in-law, Denise, was born in Le Chaux-de-Fonds, in the canton of Neuchâtel in the French-speaking part of Switzerland, and came to Britain shortly after the Second World War. She never lost her French accent (even if it did become a little eccentric over the years) and nor did she lose her taste for the Swiss way of doing things. As a result my wife's family ate Swiss cheese fondues without any of the knowing irony that eventually came to attend this fabulous dish due to the 1960s and '70s boom in cosmopolitan homeware of which the fondue set was a key part. Various retailers, most notably Habitat, successfully sold the aspiring British middle classes on the dream that they could be just as gastronomically sophisticated as their neighbours in France, Italy and Switzerland. All they had to do was buy the right kit. So everybody gave each other fondue sets until it was a cliché of the age.

The likelihood is that most people threw a fondue party once, fretted over the strange bubbling mess in the pan because it was either too thick or too thin or made with a bright orange, dull, flavourless cheese, packed it all away and never used it again. But we kept getting ours out, filling the burner with methylated spirit and making fondues, partly because it was a component of our messy family culture and partly because it is about as perfect an expression of dairy fats as you can hope to find. Oh, and it's a great way to get the kids drunk for the first time.

There is no set recipe, whatever the Internet may tell you. In Switzerland the different cantons favour different cheeses depending on what is unique to them. Generally it involves one bland cheese (the Emmental in this recipe) for bulk, and one with a stronger flavour (in this case Gruyère, but it could be something like Comté). I've seen recipes which suggest using apple juice as the liquid base, which strikes me as a terrible waste of an opportunity to cook with good wine. Don't do it like that. Do it like this.

Serves 4

1 clove of garlic
300ml good dry white wine
250g Emmental cheese
250g Gruyère cheese
1 tsp cornflour
1 tbsp kirsch (or other white firewater like Poire William.
   You could, at a push, use vodka. But DON'T use gin.
   That would be a terrible thing to do)
sea salt and ground black pepper
Dijon mustard (optional)
bread, cut into cubes
1 egg (for later)

- Cut the clove of garlic in half and rub the cut sides
  around the inside of the fondue pot.
- Place the pot on the stove and pour in the wine. Gently
  heat until it reaches a low simmer.
- Slowly mix handfuls of the cheese into the wine,
  pausing to stir until each batch has melted. This could
  take 10 to 15 minutes.
- In a small glass, mix the cornflour with the kirsch so it
  forms a paste. Dollop all of it into the fondue mix, and
  continue to stir over a low heat. After 5 minutes it
  should have thickened. If by any chance it hasn't, add
  another ½ teaspoon of cornflour (in another ½ tablespoon of spirit).
- Get a lackey to light the fondue burner on a medium
  flame.
- Now season the fondue: you can do this with just sea
  salt and black pepper to taste, though a teaspoon of
  Dijon mustard (or more if you fancy) will punch it up.
  It's your call.

- Transfer the pot immediately to the burner, and eat by spearing lumps of bread on to a fondue fork and dredging in the molten cheese. We generally eat it standing up. It's so much easier to see what's going on over the rim.
- As you get towards the bottom, much-prized crunchy bits will start to form across the enamelled surface. When there is just a bubbling mess across the bottom, crack the egg into it and beat it over the flame. Turn off the heat and scrape the last bits out. Fight the weakest family members for the best of what's left.

HOME-MADE PORK SCRATCHINGS

The industrially produced ones are boiled down in vats of fat, as I discovered on my trip to a pork-scratching factory once. It's a greasy old business. (And my pork-scratching limit is six packets in one day. It's good to know your own boundaries.) In truth this is really a recipe for pork crackling because it is baked, but the seasoning mix lifts it above and beyond something you'd have for Sunday lunch.

The good news is that many butchers will give you pig skin for free if you ask nicely, usually because they've had to take it off joints for other customers. You want the skin scored, with a good half centimetre of fat underneath. Without the fat it is just the protein of the skin. You can dry that out and deep-fry it and it will puff up into what's called chicharrón in Spain – nice if you like that sort of thing, but no scratching.

The key to this is making sure the skin is bone dry. If you have a fan oven with a defrost setting, that's perfect. Put the skin on a plate in the oven on the defrost setting and leave it for half an hour. Otherwise you'll just have to get out the hairdryer. Stop complaining. It's worth it.

2 pieces of pig skin, each 8–10cm x 15–20cm, with 0.5cm fat
   attached, ideally scored
olive oil
sea salt

For the seasoning

1 tsp smoked paprika
1 tsp fine table salt
1½ tsp caster sugar
½ tsp garlic powder
¼ tsp ground black pepper

- Preheat the oven to 220°C/425°F/gas 7.
- Flatten the pieces of dry pig skin on to an oven tray.
  Don't overcrowd them. Rub a thin film of olive oil
  across them and sprinkle over a little sea salt.
- Put into the oven. A single piece should take 30 to 40
  minutes to go crisp, but both of them may take longer,
  up to an hour. Certainly start checking after 30 minutes
  by tapping with a fork. It will go hard, and quite quickly.
  If there are bits you're unsure about and it's a cold
  winter's day, try standing outside with the oven tray in
  your hand. The sudden hit of cold air should finish the
  job. If the neighbours look at you oddly, smile back at
  them as though this is entirely reasonable behaviour.
  Because it is. This is important. We're making pork
  scratchings here.
- Mix together all the ingredients for the seasoning in a
  bowl. You can scale this recipe up. It will keep in a sealed
  container for weeks.
- When the giant scratchings (as they are now) are cool
  enough to be touched, snap them into snack-sized
  pieces.

- Get a plastic container with a lid and put the scratchings inside with a couple of teaspoons of the seasoning mix. Close the lid tightly and shake vigorously. Don't worry if you've put in too much seasoning. It will simply gather at the bottom of the box for use on the next batch.
- Try one before you serve them. Realize just how good they are, and slope off into a corner with the entire box.

6.

Thou shalt choose thy dining companions bloody carefully

I like people. Some of my best friends are people. This is helpful because, in my working life, I need them. I need people to come out to eat with me. But it's also a nightmare, as drawn in a collaboration between Munch and Brueghel, with extra pitchforks, angst and leaping flames. For when it comes to eating, the choice of dining companion is one of the most important you can make, and fraught with complications.

At first the people I invited to join me assumed I had asked them on restaurant reviews because I both appreciated their food knowledge and admired their wit. I soon put them right. I really don't care what the people who come with me think about the food, the decor or the service. They're not the ones writing the column. I am

I need them on the other side of the table so I can order enough food. To me, they are mouths connected to stomachs, at least in terms of the job I have to do. As a result, when waiters ask my table how everything is, my companions are instructed to use the word 'fine'. This isn't what they want to say, because the people I eat with are nice, which is to say nicer than me. They want to make the waiters feel good about themselves. As a result they want to babble that everything is marvellous and wonderful and frankly divine, even when the veal stew resembles the plated-up contents of a slurry pit, and the schnitzel is so tough you could walk home on it. They want to say these nice things because they are British and can't cope with confrontation. As it happens, this suits the waiters too, because they don't actually care how every-thing is. They only asked because they were told to do so; to butt in and enquire how everything is, regardless of whether the body language of the diners bellows 'go-away-we're-having-a-moment' or not.

The word 'fine' may seem unnecessarily passive-aggressive, but it leaves me room for manoeuvre. I need that. If the people I'm with say everything is marvellous and then I write a negative review, it causes pursed lips and clenched fists among the staff of the restaurant involved, and not unreasonably so: 'On the night you were here your table told us everything was fabulous. And now: look at the blood you have spilled in words and punctuation marks.'

The word 'fine' covers a multitude of sins. It leaves the restaur-ant none the wiser. It leaves me space in which to work out what I think about a restaurant, because sometimes pinning down exactly what's right or what's wrong can take time. I am very deep and thoughtful.

Also, I am a bit lazy.

Deciding what I think about the people I am with is a different matter entirely. That, I can do very quickly indeed, which is good because it really is important. From time to time I am asked to name my favourite restaurant experience. I know what answer is hoped for. I am meant to talk about that amazing place where they did the thing with the turbot and the caviar and the bucket of butter, or that other place with the wood-fired grill, where the steaks take you back to your Palaeolithic self. But this is to miss the point, because a great restaurant experience isn't just about the cooking and the cutlery and the room and the service. Or even about these things at all.

It's really about who you are with, and you have to choose them with great care. God save me from a dinner with those nap-kin sniffers who want only to talk about the food on the plate in front of them; who want to dissect every collection of ingredients as if it held some secret to existence, which it never does. I love restaurants not just because I am greedy, though I am, but because they are the perfect setting in which to unpick life's filthy truths. Choose the right dining companion, one sodden with regrets and victories, secrets and headlines, in equal measure, and a good dinner becomes a journey into the heart of what it is to be human.

Get that bit wrong, and dinner will be a disaster, as I have found out to my cost. From time to time I auction off my companion slot on a review for charity. It baffles me why anybody wants to pay money for the experience. All they will see is a middle-aged man with too much hair, ordering food and eating it. There's nothing to witness, no process or mechanics. I do not winch a spectrometer down from the ceiling to inspect the ingredients, or get out colour charts to verify the shade of the carrots. I do not have a score system of the sort used by Accident and Emergency doctors to discern the level of pain you're experiencing. It's just me sat on my large arse, eating and occasionally rolling my eyes. But hey, if it raises money for charity so be it.

The problem is that in the age of the Internet the people who turn up can be rather random. In the old days when print ruled supreme, the people who read my column did so by buying the whole newspaper. As a result they generally shared its values and, by extension, mine. Now it's possible to read my column online without ever going anywhere near the rest of the newspaper. Some of these people can end up sharing my values in the way lions share a zebra on the African plains. Given half a chance they will happily dismember them.

An example: a few years ago, I was purchased by the wife of an oil trader. This is an extremely reductive way to define anybody, but it was the way she defined herself. She lived in southern Spain, read my column from there, and wanted to meet me. I took her to a very nice Middle Eastern-influenced restaurant and set about making small talk. It was talk so small, you would have needed an electron microscope to identify it. Which is why it was so startling when, halfway through the main course, she leaned towards me and said, 'Shall I tell you why Margaret Thatcher is a hero of mine?'

No, I said. Please don't. You may have bought me for charity but I write for a left-of-centre newspaper for a reason. I really don't want to hear why you idolize Margaret Thatcher. I would rather be served a salad made with my own toe clippings. It put me right off my shawarma.

If only it was just disagreements over politics. I know how to shut down conversations about politics. The fact is that, when it comes to eating in restaurants, there are just so many problems with other people.

For example, I fully understand that making choices in life can be tricky: what career to pursue, so you don't end up wanting to saw off your own leg with frustration within a year; which person to go to bed with, so you don't find yourself sharing dampened sheets with somebody who, when you've finished all the oohing and squelching, decides to tell you they think Hermann Goering was a little misunderstood and had some pretty cool ideas, actually.

However, choosing what to eat off a menu in a restaurant is never tricky. It's not complicated. It's not like filing a tax return or getting North Korea to see sense. It's simple. There's a list of dishes. You read the list and choose the one that sounds nicest or, at a push, least nasty. I spend an absurd amount of my working life in restaurants, choosing things off lists, and cannot help but marvel at the people who, asked what they would like to eat, flap their hands about like they're shooing away flies and mutter, 'Ooh, come back to me last.' Why? What are you waiting for? Divine intervention? A scorching column of light to descend from the heavens to illuminate the place on the sheet where it says 'rump of lamb with aubergine puree and boulangère potatoes', the bloody dish that we all knew you were going to order anyway?

There is a simple truth. People who take ages trying to choose what to eat in restaurants don't really like food. Not enough, anyway. They can't choose because they are suspicious of what it is exactly the kitchen might be attempting to do to them. For them every dish is an elephant trap, specifically designed to make them look like the picky eater we all know they are. And don't even try suggesting it's because menus are full of too many lovely things to make a simple choice possible. I read more menus than you do. I have measured out my life in badly punctuated starters and grammatically incorrect mains. And I can tell you that the number packed full of glorious possibilities can be counted on the fingers of my left hand. After I've put fingers one to four through a threshing machine.

Menu choices are simple. You go out wanting the fish or the steak. That's the kind of person you are. Or at least that's the kind of person you are tonight. You may think yourself a deeply discerning person, but really you have made this decision before you arrive. You turn up, look down the list, find the thing that most closely approximates how you're feeling and you choose it. If I were allowed to order like that, we all know what would happen. I'd order the pork belly and pull my 'so shoot me' face at anyone who rolls their eyes.

I'm not allowed to do that. I have to find the thing that reads most like a car crash full of mangled body parts: the deconstructed prawn cocktail with Marie Rose ice cream and iceberg lettuce jelly; the sweetbreads with the amaretto velouté (both real examples). And if there aren't any of those, I have to find the thing that looks complicated. And if there is neither of those I get to choose the thing that sounds nice which isn't pork belly. I can do all that in about ninety seconds, leaving the rest of the time free to force people to laugh at my crap jokes. That's just how people who really like their food work.

I have the same problem with people who eat slowly. Whenever I find myself at a table with someone lacking what I regard as the necessary velocity around food, I become transfixed. How does it work, this slow-eating thing? The tedious grind of knife against meat, the endless roll of molar across muscle fibre, the huge yawning gaps between mouthfuls? It's wrong. It's unnatural. What's most striking is how unconscious of the fact slow eaters generally are. Sitting in a restaurant with a party of six, they never seem to notice that the rest of their party are stabbing themselves in the back of the hand with forks, or fixing nooses to the light fittings, while they poke away laboriously at whatever plateful they have ordered. They don't notice that they are holding everyone up.

Of course, sometimes this issue around eating arises with age and illness. My parents both lived to a fair old age, and both of them experienced this problem, which they found acutely frustrating because, unsurprisingly, they were as greedy as me. It's the other people, the ones without the excuses, who drive me nuts. I've tried asking slow eaters about their bad habits, but the answer is rarely satisfying. Sometimes they look baffled, which is probably down to a lack of nutrition interfering with cognitive ability. Sometimes they claim it's healthier. Which it isn't. As long as it's not a 400-hot-dogs-in-half-an-hour eating contest, it makes no difference whether you clear your plate in ten minutes or forty. Indeed, eating slowly could actually be detrimental to their health. Because I might eventually lose patience, lunge across the table and ram the damn fork into the roof of their mouth.

The worst are those who smugly tell you they eat slowly because they like to savour their food. The verb 'to savour' is foul. It's sodden with judgement, swollen with its own self-importance. It's language with its nose in the air: I savour; he bolts; you gorge. If you don't savour, if you too don't eat slowly, they are saying, it is because you are in the grip of the second deadly sin: gluttony. And it's only a short hop and skip from there to the other black marks, like sloth and lust.

In this regard those who claim they like to savour their food are bang on. For here is the truth about us fast eaters. We like life more than slow eaters like life. Slow eaters aren't just doing something they love more slowly than others are doing it. Again, they simply don't like food, not enough. No one with a real instinct to feed and be fed can ever eat slowly. Call those of us who rampage through a plate of food like floodwater through a sluice gate greedy if you wish, but if fast eating leads in turn to lust and then sloth, well, that sounds like a bloody good night out to me. For that's the point. Greedy people are enthusiasts. They are there to suck the marrow from the roasted thigh bone of life. We recognize our appetites in all their forms and, unlike the buttoned-up, repressed, spank-me-now-and-call-me Alice slow eaters, we are not ashamed of our true natures.

Sure, eating fast has its downsides. We end up with empty plates more quickly. That which we have so adored is gone so terribly quickly. Fast eating brings with it a profound sense of loss. But that's all right. That's okay. Because life is there to be lived, and the best moments cannot be drawn out artificially.

While I'm about it, save me from people who regard a menu as merely the opening position in a protracted negotiation, who want that element left out, and this bit on the side. If you don't want to eat any of these dishes, why did you come here? There are also people who eat with their mouths open and people who drag their cutlery across the porcelain. Can't stand either of them. And then there are the people who order their steak well done. Why do that? Because there really is no point taking the life of an animal if all you are going to do is completely ruin it the moment you get it near the fire. Asking for your steak well done is a crime against food.

A well-done steak is not a sweet affectation. It's a violation. And yes, I know I'm ranting, but this is important. Why in God's name would anyone want to take a good piece of meat and cook it until it has the texture of a school satchel, but none of the utility? Why would they want to put something in their mouth that tastes of nothing and gives your jaw cramps? Why would they want to rob it of the very thing that makes it itself? Those of us who eat meat should face up to what it once was: a living creature that bled if it was pricked and can bleed still. We should eat it because we like the flavour, and a significant amount of that lies in its juices.

There are some who would say this is just snobbery. To which, as ever, I say: what do you mean, just? Snobbery is good. Snobbery is terrific. Snobbery is what makes the world move forward. Without snobbery we'd still be buying olive oil from the chemist's and using it to cure earache. We'd still be thinking Vesta ready meals were a neat idea, drinking Blue Nun, squirting cream from a can, and incinerating our steaks because meat with the blush of blood is what those funny foreign people across the Channel like to eat. Snobs are in the vanguard.

Show me someone who likes their meat overcooked and I will show you a picky eater, who regards mealtimes as a set of challenges and insults to be negotiated, like oil-slicked chicanes on a racetrack. The well-done steak is a mark of a life unlived, of a childish world view retained. Of a distinct fearfulness. Talk to someone who insists on having their meat incinerated and eventually they will mutter about contagion and sickness, as if eating were really a game of Russian roulette. And yes, of course, certain things do need to be cooked through; I am not eating chicken tartare made from a bird that originated in the British flock any day soon. But with beef or lamb or venison, duck or grouse, and even with pork these days, serving it rare so the juices run is not a quick route to the nearest cemetery. It is not suicide by dinner. It is a quick route to a good meal. Perhaps you still can't stomach the idea. Maybe the sight of pink flesh makes you heave. In which case you really shouldn't be eating meat at all. You don't deserve it.

Perhaps you regard all this as horribly bigoted. I see it as no more than a modest proposal. Indeed, when it comes to dining companions, I'm really not that picky at all. As long as they order quickly, don't haggle over the menu, don't take hours to eat, do so with their mouth closed and their knife edge off the plate, and only order meat no more cooked than medium rare, everything should be fine.

All of this deals with our conscious responses to dining companions. A growing body of research suggests that who we eat with can also, unconsciously, have a big influence on our behaviour. For example, a 2012 study by a team of psychologists at Radboud University, Nijmegen, in the Netherlands, found that women tended to mimic the appetites of each other in social situations. A woman eating with a light-eating woman (instructed to do so as part of the study) would eat almost exactly the same amount of food; likewise, a woman eating with another who was stuffing their face would do the same. Why? The researchers theorized that, at an unconscious level, women are desperate to conform to each other's modes of behaviour.

Behaviour can even be influenced by the size of the dining companion. A 2014 study from the journal *Appetite* invited a mixed group of diners to serve themselves from a buffet. In front of them, serving herself, was an actress. When she wore a fat suit to make her look obese, the subjects served themselves more food than when she was her normal slender self. It didn't matter what she actually put on her plate. Just the sight of her inflated self was enough to make them pile up the food.

Another piece of research found that if the diners are men, eating with women, it didn't even take a fat suit to get them to consume more. According to a 2015 study conducted at Cornell University and published in the journal *Evolutionary Psychological Science*, when men eat with women they are driven to eat substantially more. Diners were monitored as they served themselves from a pizza and salad bar, and then invited to choose who they would like to eat with. The men who sat down exclusively with women ate over 90 per cent more pizza and over 85 per cent more salad than the men who ate with other men. This may be because men are hard-wired to prove their machismo, and will do so with whatever is to hand. If this means stuffing their faces, then so be it.

Also, men are utter knobs.

*

There is one obvious solution to the problem of choosing your dining companion: don't bother. Eat by yourself. I know that eating alone, like trainspotting and stalking celebrities, gets a bad press. It's regarded as a sad pursuit for sad people with tragic lives and a touch of halitosis – and it's easy to see why. Here is a dispatch from the very front line of solo eating, and it ain't pretty. It was a winter's night in Birmingham circa 1994 and I had just pulled off a journalistic coup – something to do with the intelligence services and dodgy photographs – and I wanted to reward myself. Obviously a reward meant food, so I called an Italian, recommended by a local listings mag, and cheerfully asked for a table for one. There was a snigger from the end of the line, a brisk 'Not tonight, sir', and then they hung up.

I stared baffled at the receiver, before pushing on. I called a Chinese place and got a similar response, and some French bistro in Edgbaston, before, in desperation, calling the American-style brasserie that even the dodgy local listings mag seemed to hate. There was a sharp intake of breath. 'Trying to book a table for one on Valentine's night, mate? That's tough.' I hadn't noticed the date.

I ended up in the restaurant of the Holiday Inn in Birmingham where I was staying, eating the breast of a duck that had probably died sometime in the decade before last, of natural causes. As I entered the restaurant, the man in charge – maître d' would be pushing it, and we both knew it – said, 'And would sir care for a magazine?' The only other time that happened to me was in the treatment rooms of a high-end fertility clinic, where at least they had something I actually wanted to read.

It's all there, isn't it: the pathos, the rejection, the funereal pall. The remarkable thing about this experience, however, is that it did not put me off. All it did was convince me that, while eating alone can be a wonderful thing, the circumstances have to be right. That evening they simply weren't. Here is what you need to know. As with any other solo pursuit, eating alone requires a carefully balanced combination of commitment, enthusiasm and self-adoration.

It should, after all, be a meal with someone you love. Hell, if you go out for dinner by yourself and discover you don't like the company, you really are in trouble. So you need to be in a good mood. I regard myself as a gregarious man. I like people and their chatter but sometimes the conversation I really want is the one with myself – we never disagree, me and I – and that happens best over food.

As a restaurant critic I have often eaten alone, usually weekday lunches out of London when none of my friends who have proper jobs can join me. I will confess that on these occasions I tend to book a table for two and then announce when I arrive that there will just be one diner. This is not out of embarrassment; I don't care whether people think I'm a knobby-no-mates. It's simply that British restaurateurs regard single diners suspiciously, start wondering if we're Michelin inspectors or sociopaths or both, and who needs that?

So I go and I consider the menu and the room. But most of all I study the other people, watch their body language, listen in to their conversations. When I eat alone I have a licence to snoop. Once, in the grand dining room of an Eastbourne hotel, I heard a dignified, elegant couple explaining to their adult children that the space in which we were all eating had long ago been their apartment. 'You, darling, were conceived over there,' the mother said to one of her sons, pointing at where the cheese trolley loitered, and we all turned to look, as if we might just catch them going at it, across the creamy reblochon.

Sometimes I take a book, and lose myself in the rhythm of the food and the words and the wine and the words and the words and the wine. Downing a bottle at home on the sofa by yourself is, if not exactly sad, hardly glamorous. Doing the same over an impeccable côte de boeuf and crème brûlée, with a slab of Philip Roth or Stieg Larsson for company, has about it the authentic whiff of adulthood. It says: I am a grown-up. I have taste. I like myself. Now piss off and leave me in peace.

*

Sometimes getting rid of everyone is impossible. And sometimes, we do all make the wrong choice of dining companion. Occasionally they become the wrong choice halfway through the meal. Three glasses of Gamay down, the sweet, interesting, dynamic soul on the other side of the table becomes a self-absorbed misanthrope, who hates everybody and everything and is going to tell you why in excruciating detail.

In these circumstances there is only one thing for it: dessert.

At the end of a terrible night in a restaurant, dessert can be your friend, partly because the arrival of the dessert menu is a sign that the ordeal is almost over, and partly because it is an indulgence you have earned. The fact is nobody ever needs dessert. It is always an exercise in superfluity. Let's be honest: few of us actually go to restaurants to deal with hunger. We go for the occasion, for the experience, for the people. Indeed, often we make ourselves hungry so we can do the restaurant justice. We miss lunch because we know we're eating dinner out. We go for a run as preparation, like a boxer limbering up for a championship bout. But when we finally get there the food we actually need to sate that hunger is the savoury stuff. No one has ever turned up at a restaurant, declared they're starving and announced they have to have the white chocolate parfait. (Some people might have wanted to do so, but that's a different matter.)

Dessert is the indulgence we squeeze in. What's more, while the savoury parts of the meal can be executed by technicians, it takes a properly greedy person to write a good dessert menu. It has to be written by someone well versed in the language of 'wants' rather than 'needs'.

The recipe here is most definitely a want. It really is completely superfluous. But you may wish to deploy it strategically, perhaps when you have been forced to invite people you hate around to dinner. The arrival of this on the table is the sign you have been waiting for.

The ordeal is over. This is your reward.

CHOCOLATE PUDDING WITH CHERRIES AND
RED WINE SAUCE

This is a straightforward twist on a classic baked chocolate pudding, which takes its cue from Black Forest gateau by adding cherries, and, in the process, producing its own sauce.

Serves 4

250ml red wine
140g caster sugar
around 20 fresh cherries, stoned (halve them if it's easier)
150g dark chocolate, broken into pieces
115g butter, plus extra for greasing
2 large eggs
1tsp vanilla extract
25g plain flour
cream, to serve

- Put the red wine, 3 tablespoons of the sugar and the cherries into a small pan over a medium heat. When it starts to boil, turn the heat down and simmer for 20 minutes.
- Strain the cherries with a sieve, reserving the wine. Let the cherries cool and dry in the sieve. Meanwhile, put the wine back into the pan over a medium heat and reduce by half until it's starting to go syrupy. Allow to cool.
- To make the pudding, melt the chocolate and butter together in a heatproof bowl over a simmering pan of water. When melted, give it a good stir to mix it all together fully.
- In a large bowl, whisk together the remaining sugar and the eggs with the vanilla extract until thick and foamy. Carefully fold the chocolate mixture into the egg

mixture. Now sieve the flour over the chocolate mixture and fold in carefully.

- Set the oven to 190°C/375°F/gas 5. Butter the inside of four small ramekins.
- Put four or five of the cherries into the bottom of each ramekin. Pour over the chocolate pudding mix.
- Bake in the oven for 20 to 25 minutes. It's ready when there is still a slight wobble in the middle when you nudge the ramekin. Serve immediately with cream and the red wine sauce.

Now write a love letter thanking me.

7.

Thou shalt not sneer at meat-free cookery

A weekday lunchtime and I am standing by my stove again, doing something appalling. I have done bad things with food before, of course. I once ate two Pot Noodles for dinner, and didn't even feel guilty. It was a long time ago, but I did it. I have ordered wings from the very cheapest fried-rat inner-city chicken shop and scarfed confectionery that has first been battered and deep-fried in a Glasgow chip shop. I have eaten a pizza with twelve mini-cheeseburgers around the crust, at Pizza Hut. All of these things are shameful, but they have a redeeming feature which is that they are in keeping with my flawed character. I am a man of appetites and sometimes those appetites make me do things. You cannot have one part of me without the other.

What I am doing now is not in character. It goes against everything in which I believe. But still I am doing it because, if I'm going to make a convincing argument about what non-meat cookery should and shouldn't look like, I first have to go to the very darkest of places. I have to stand in another person's shoes.

And so: I am cooking with Quorn. I am cooking with a meat substitute, made using a fungal growth called mycoprotein, which is meant to have a meaty texture that recalls the muscle mass of something which once had a pulse.

I am doing this properly. By the manufacturer's own admission Quorn doesn't taste of much unless introduced to other flavours, so first I am making a tomato sauce: chopped onions and garlic cooked down in glugs of olive oil with a tin of good tomatoes, and generous amounts of salt and black pepper. I let it simmer. I treat it as I would any tomato sauce that is going to a good home, even though I suspect this one isn't. I blitz it, season again, and then cook it out until it starts to separate slightly. In another pan I fry off some cubes of Quorn™ Meat Free Chicken Pieces. The pedant in me fumes quietly at the lack of inverted commas around the reference to chicken, the exclusion of which I regard as bad manners. It is chicken in the same way as I am George Clooney. But no matter. Their product, their rules. I do as I'm told and sauté these eager-to-please little squares until they've started to colour, and wonder whether this might be an approximation of the Maillard reaction, the caramelization of meat which gives it that savouriness carnivores like me crave so desperately. I try a piece. It isn't. It tastes like slightly crunchy overused mattress filling. It really does need that sauce.

So I give it sauce, a big dollop of the stuff. The remaining sauce receives a couple of handfuls of the mince. Or 'mince'. I turn down the heat to a simmer, and wander off to play the piano, hoping a couple of choruses of something cheerful like 'Moanin'' or 'Mean to Me' will soothe the disquiet.

Eventually, despite my willing it otherwise, the cooking is done. The food must be tasted. I stand by the stove and fork them both away, regarding neither as worth dirtying a plate for. I close my lips and press the pieces of mock meat against the roof of my mouth and stare sadly at the pans.

I could now lurch into hyperbole. I could rant on about this piece of cookery being where both hope and calories go to die; I could describe it as a culinary nightmare of which Freddie Krueger would be proud. I could say I would prefer to have my tongue lacerated by a threshing machine, or spend nine hours in a lift with Donald Trump, or have hot wax painted on to my genitals. But I won't, because these Quorn dishes are so much worse than that.

They are dull. They are nothing, a tiny belch of mediocrity. No, eating them isn't a demonstration of the gag reflex. I'm not scanning the room desperately, looking for someone who might be willing to hold back my hair should the need arise. I am just depressed. These fragments of tortured fungus do have a texture. They bounce and vibrate beneath the teeth, and I suppose if you were sufficiently with the project you might, if the wind were blowing in the right direction, and your hormone levels were set to optimum, recognize a similarity to meat.

But why bother? Really. Why choose to eat something like this? If you don't want to eat meat, why bother trying to eat something which is a sad, inoffensive, bland approximation of a shadow of meat's distant relative? Why go to all that trouble? What made me most mad about all this, however, wasn't just the dreary eating experience. It was the damage it's done. Because this plateful of tiresome, boring sludge has simply given ammunition to those militant carnivores who spit and laugh in the face of non-meat cookery. It really is lousy PR for the cause of the vegetable.

And, as we edge ever deeper into the twenty-first century, that is something we simply cannot afford.

I have watched animals die. I have stood at the head of the kill line in an abattoir and looked on as the electric shocks were administered, a paddle pressed to each side of the skull, followed by a blade to the throat. I have seen the speed at which the blood bursts from a body, hinged between life and death. Species changes everything. The death of a beef animal, hung twelve feet from the ceiling by a chain around its leg, is more striking than the death of a sheep, which hangs low and face to face with the slaughter man behind his spattered visor.

Dying pigs do squeal.

When I went to the abattoir a few years ago I interrogated my motives. I was writing a chapter about the environmental impact of meat consumption for a new book, and felt that describing the process by which animals die to feed us would be the most striking way into the subject. But there was something else too. Some people have a problem with the killing of sentient creatures for food. I had always said that I did not. I never had done. As far as I could see, these animals existed in the first place only because we brought them into the world to be eaten. This would be problematical only if you viewed animals in some way as our equals and, while some people do hold this view, again, I did not. As long as the animal had had both a good life and a good death, all was fine.

While I believed this, I also wondered if it wasn't a bit glib. It's all well and good to structure a nice argument. But what if you actually had to watch animals die? What then? Would that change things? I wanted to test my attitudes in the face of brutal realities. In truth I had wanted to go further. I had explored the possibility of doing the killing myself, but getting the licences and permissions to do so is, rightly, complicated. There are many jobs in an abattoir; actually slaughtering animals stands right at the top of the hierarchy in terms of status and respect. It was not something I could get to do. Watching close up, again and again and again, was very much the next best thing. By which I mean the very worst.

And the result? It didn't change my views one bit.

I left the abattoir holding the same opinions as I did when I arrived, albeit in need of a stiff drink. I have argued piously that all meat eaters ought to be prepared to go inside a slaughterhouse. If you want to eat animals you should be willing to know what that means. And I do think that sort of experience would be hugely beneficial to the conversation we need to keep having about what and how we eat now. Perhaps you could acquire a carnivore's licence only once you had spent a day in an abattoir. That said, I suspect the vast majority of people would come out with their views little changed. Or even if they swore off meat for a while, the vast majority would eventually drift back, probably lured there by the smell of a bacon sandwich, properly made. The eating of meat is simply that ingrained.

Diehard carnivores like to argue this is because humans have a physiological need for meat. It's true, as studies have found, that we will declare ourselves sated as a result of eating fewer calories of meat than, say, vegetables. It is an exceptionally efficient source of nutrition. There is also much evidence that eating meat many thousands of years ago enabled our ancestors to develop the kind of intellectual capacity that eventually made us human; indeed human enough for some of us to choose to be vegan. Foraged leaves, nuts and berries took too much energy to digest for the brain of prehistoric man to get what it needed. Meat simply allowed us to obtain the volume of protein needed for the human brain to become itself.

That said, the anthropologist Richard Wrangham has argued convincingly in his book *Catching Fire: How Cooking Made Us Human* that the really important development was not the eating of meat alone, but the use of fire to cook foods generally (including vegetables), making them all easier to digest and so releasing more nutrition. In his book *The Diet Myth*, Tim Spector, Professor of Genetic Epidemiology at King's College London, notes that non-meat eaters can be afflicted by a vitamin B12 deficiency, which has many impacts, including possible neurological dysfunction. During his own personal experiments with veganism, Spector became deficient in B12. He tried taking supplements, but that didn't improve his levels so he resorted to intramuscular injections in his bottom. He eventually concluded it was too radical an approach. 'This is daft,' he wrote. 'I am trying to be fit and healthy yet having injections every month feels neither healthy nor particularly natural.' He solved the problem by eating steak once or twice a month. His vitamin levels returned to normal. This story will not be appreciated by the vegan community.

Whatever the arguments over whether modern man actually needs meat, eating it certainly remains an ingrained part of the human culture. In his 1991 book, *Meat: A Natural Symbol*, the academic Nick Fiddes quotes anthropological studies of various primitive tribes which found they used different language to describe being hungry for meat as distinct from being simply hungry. Elsewhere he talks about how, in Uganda, a man would trade a volume of plantain that would feed his family for four days for a scrawny chicken that, by comparison, had very little calorific value. The chicken might be less nutritious, but it was still highly prized for what it represented.

Fiddes, ever the structuralist, concludes that eating meat 'tangibly represents human control of the natural world. Consuming the muscle flesh of other highly evolved animals is a potent statement of our supreme power.' As he says elsewhere, 'Taste is not an absolute. It is something we develop while growing up within a culture which has its own general preferences.' We all know the latter to be true. Some of us like spicy food and some do not. Some of us like oysters slurped raw off the half shell and some do not. So no, meat eating, however efficient a supply of protein it might be for us, may not be an imperative. It is a deep-seated cultural choice which says a lot about our position of power in the world. Certainly, the more powerful we become, the more we tend to eat it. Numerous studies have shown that the higher up the income ladder we rise, the more meat we eat, and not simply because it's costly stuff (for it becomes affordable at quite a low point on that income ladder). In China the emergence of the middle classes can be measured in meat consumption, from 10kg per person per year in 1975 to 45kg by 2012, with a forecast of 69kg by 2030 (as meat consumption in the US and UK slips down from a peak of around 80kg per person per year).

Meat has long been a symbol of power. In William Hogarth's 1748 painting originally entitled *The Gate of Calais*, a huge piece of beef is shown being transported to an English tavern, while undernourished French soldiers look on. The painting, now held by Tate Britain in London, became known as *O the Roast Beef of Old England* and took on the role of a blunt piece of propaganda, the power of the English represented by their hearty diet of dead cow.

Eventually, of course, the French caught up and, through the books and teachings of chef Marie-Antoine Carême in the early nineteenth century and Auguste Escoffier in the late nineteenth and early twentieth century, created a culinary repertoire that put meat front and centre, literally. Any chef going through a French classical training has long been taught to start with a lump of animal protein in the centre of the plate and build out from there. In the late 1990s the Israeli-born chef, restaurateur and writer Yotam Ottolenghi arrived in London and signed up for a six-month course at the Cordon Bleu cookery school. 'It was always about the meat,' he says now. 'Everything else on the plate was in service of the meat or fish. I have never cooked as much meat as I did during those six months.'

If ever there were a symbol of that, it would be the existence of that Quorn I cooked with so reluctantly. Why would we have desperate meat substitutes, if not for the cultural primacy of the meat they are trying to replace? They are based on the assumption that if a vegetable-led menu is going to succeed, it has to ape flesh. And that's exactly why meat substitutes fail so spectacularly. For non-meat cookery to be successful it has to do so according to its own agenda, not according to one set by that which it is replacing.

Happily, things are changing, albeit by necessity. There is finally an understanding of the environmental impact of raising livestock for consumption, especially when they are fed on crops that could be fed directly to humans rather more efficiently. There are varying figures depending on species, with cattle requiring the most grain and chickens the least, but on average it takes five kilos of grain to produce one kilo of meat. With the global population rising from just north of 7 billion now, towards 10 billion or even more by the end of the century, we cannot afford to be stuffing all those crops down the gullets of animals. And then there's the carbon footprint. One study by the United Nations Food and Agriculture Organization attributed 18 per cent of all greenhouse-gas emissions to the livestock industry. This figure has been disputed. Simon Fairlie, author of *Meat: A Benign Extravagance*, points out that the UNFAO figure attributes literally all deforestation globally to the meat business. And yet significant amounts are down to logging and land development. He puts the proportion of greenhouse-gas emissions at closer to 10 per cent, though he accepts that this is still too much.

While some diehard opponents of the meat business argue (and will always argue) that all of it is an unnecessary use of land upon which crops could be grown for human consumption, Fairlie notes that ruminants eat a lot of biomass that cannot be consumed by humans and which would otherwise be wasted, and can be grazed on upland fields which cannot be used for crops. Once he does all his sums, Fairlie concludes that our meat consumption needs to fall to about half of what it is now. Which it almost certainly will do anyway, because meat prices are going to continue rising alongside demand from the emerging middle classes in Asia. There is a limit to production, not just in terms of desirability, but also in practicality.

Which means one thing. The future of non-meat cookery is not in the hands of those who have sworn off eating animals altogether. It's in the hands of those of us who are cutting down. Or the reductarians, as some have called themselves and I never will, because it's the sort of contrived word which makes me want to punch walls. It also smacks of doctrine and manifesto, a defining feature of the radical meat-free lobby. Suggesting people might like to try cutting down is a different, much gentler approach. It is about good taste and good sense rather than cant.

The abomination that is meat-free sausages and burgers wasn't created by meat eaters looking for something that wasn't meat but almost looked like it. It was created by vegetarians who believed this to be the only way to advance their cause and who, in any case, don't especially like the real thing and so don't really care that it's horrid. They are the same people responsible for vegetarian moussakas and cottage pies, dishes which are an apology for themselves. These are dishes which are trying (and failing) to be good in spite of the fact they don't include meat. A moussaka requires the slaughter of a lamb to be moussaka. A cottage pie requires ground beef. A sausage exists as a way to use up every inch of the pig, including its intestines. Something formed out of oats and soya and desperation is not a sausage. It's a lack of imagination on a plate.

Non-meat cookery needs to be good because of that fact. The best non-meat cookery does not have a meaty twin. It's not an echo of the real thing, the recipe contrived by substitutions and arch compromise and regret. It is itself. There is, for example, nothing with a pulse which will improve a perfectly made wild mushroom risotto: rice, wine, stock, mushrooms, cheese and the job is done. The entirely meat-free curries of the Gujarat would not be better if only somebody could be fagged to kill a chicken. A tabbouleh, full of the vigour of flat-leaf parsley, lemon juice and cracked wheat, isn't begging to be augmented by the addition of roast pork.

Ambitious restaurants in Britain and elsewhere have, in recent years, started filling their menus with these non-meat-based dishes, and for the most part the movement has been led by meat-eating multi-starred chefs – the likes of Simon Rogan at L'Enclume and Brett Graham at the Ledbury. The latter has a completely meat-free tasting menu. 'It's a good thing that it's meat-eating chefs who have led this rather than the vegetarian hard core,' Yotam Ottolenghi says. 'There's been a reversal of the ingredient hierarchy and we've helped to normalize it. ' A humble vegetable like the cauliflower, which spent the entirety of the 1970s in Britain being tortured in boiling water until it surrendered both its nutritional value and dignity, has become a centrepiece. At Berber & Q, a charcoal grill house in London's Hackney, it is roasted whole and served with tahini and pomegranate seeds, and holds its own on a menu alongside dishes of slow-roasted beef short rib or lamb shawarma. At Palomar, the London outpost of an Israeli restaurant group, it is flamed on the Josper grill with lemon butter, and served with their own labneh – fresh cheese – and toasted almonds. At Ottolenghi's restaurant Nopi, it comes roasted with saffron, sultanas and crispy capers.

The Middle Eastern influence is obvious, but the movement is far broader than that. Chef Robin Gill spent his early years working for Marco Pierre White, when he was in his multi-Michelin-starred French classical pomp at the Oak Room restaurant of Le Méridien Hotel on London's Piccadilly. 'There, it was completely protein-led,' Gill says. 'It was all about foie gras, fillet steak and truffles.' It was the kind of kitchen where they would roast whole chickens, solely to make jus, and then throw the meat away. Gill's approach was changed by a stint in southern Italy, where he says the beef was terrible but the vegetables brilliant. That was followed by time at Raymond Blanc's Le Manoir aux Quat'Saisons in Oxfordshire, which, for all its commitment to French classicism, has a vast kitchen garden on-site.

Later, Gill opened his own restaurant, the Dairy, in south London, followed by the nearby Manor and then Paradise Garage in east London. At all three the menu walks both sides of the line. Sure, it serves meat. But it's also about dishes of carrots with roasted barley and sorrel, or salsify with smoked curd and pickled walnuts; it's about beetroot with fermented apple and pine, or charred leeks with caramelized Comté cheese and wild garlic. These are dish descriptions which make their own case. 'My mindset has simply changed,' Gill says. 'I don't feel the need for a lump of beef in the middle of the plate.'

And vegetarian sausages? 'I don't get them at all. They're pointless. It's the kind of stuff that really annoys me. It's food created by people who can't cook.'

It's a rude thing to say. It's also probably a little unfair. But sod it, I'm not going to argue.

POT-ROASTED CAULIFLOWER

Yet another dish elevating the once-humble cauliflower. A version of this was shown to me by René Redzepi, chef of Noma in Copenhagen, acclaimed for its highly regional Nordic agenda, the menu of which features many non-meat dishes. His version used yoghurt whey for the acidity of the dressing, but that's not something a lot of us have to hand. This version is simpler and produces more caramelization.

Serves 2 as a main course, or more as a side dish

1 whole head of cauliflower
25g unsalted butter
1 tbsp white wine vinegar
2 tbsp water
a sprig of fresh rosemary, or, failing that, 1 tsp dried herbs
sea salt

- Remove the leaves from the cauliflower, then slice across the bottom to produce a flat base. Now slice it in half vertically.
- Melt the butter in a solid cooking pot with a lid, big enough to take the whole cauliflower. When it's melted, put the cauliflower flat-bottom down on to the bubbling butter. Put the sprig of rosemary on the top, or if you're using dried herbs, sprinkle these around the base.
- Put the lid on, turn the heat to medium and leave for 20 minutes.
- The base should now be nicely caramelized. Turn the cauliflower so the flat sides where you cut it in half vertically are at the bottom of the pot. Put the lid back on and cook for another 15 minutes.
- Remove the cauliflower to a warmed serving bowl, caramelized sides up. Mix the vinegar with the water.

Take the pot off the heat and deglaze it with the vinegar mixture, scraping at the crusty bits with a wooden spoon.
- Pour the liquor over the cauliflower and season with sea salt.

LEEKS VINAIGRETTE

There are indeed lots of modern ways to cook with vegetables and lots of exotic influences to be brought to the table. But there is always a place for a simple but graceful old stager like this. The key to this is to make sure the leeks have drained completely.

Serves 4 as a starter, or 2 as a Sunday-night supper

3 medium-sized leeks
1 egg
200ml vinaigrette (see page 10)
sea salt and ground black pepper
optional: 4 tbsp chopped capers and cornichons, to garnish

- Wash the leeks. Trim the bases and the green tops, reserving them for soup because you're a good person who doesn't shamelessly waste stuff like that. Slice the leeks into three equal pieces across the width. (Note: a lot of recipes suggest keeping the leeks in one piece by slicing down to within a couple of couple of inches of the base. My method is more fiddly because you end up trying to keep the pieces of leek together, but it does mean the finished dish is less waterlogged and easier to eat.)
- Simmer in boiling water for around 10 minutes, until soft to the tip of a knife. Drain and leave to cool.
- In the meantime, place the egg in cold water, bring to the boil, then continue boiling for 3 minutes, so that the egg is set but still a little soft. Set aside to cool.
- When the leeks are cool enough to handle, carefully

slice each piece in half lengthways. Put a couple of layers of kitchen paper on a plate and, taking care to keep each piece of leek together, lay them out, cut-side down, on the paper to continue draining for another half an hour.

- To serve: still taking care to keep them together, place the leeks in a single layer, cut-side down, in a serving dish. Dress with the vinaigrette. Peel the egg and roughly crush with a fork, mixing the crumbled yolk into the white. Sprinkle over the leeks, then season with sea salt and ground black pepper.
- Sprinkle with the chopped capers and cornichons, if using.

8.

Thou shalt celebrate the stinky

Given the build-up, the delivery was a bit of an anticlimax. The website I'd purchased the item from had been splattered with warnings, like I was entering some dodgy nuclear power installation at my own risk. They could deliver only within Britain, they said, because most airlines wouldn't allow what I wanted on-board. There was a darker warning that they couldn't even guarantee availability outside of the summer months. The thing I wanted was only to be opened al fresco, where the winds blow. It had originated in Sweden (presumably then brought to Britain overland), and in Sweden you have to wait for summer for such outdoor pursuits, because the winters are too cold.

But praise be, despite it being January, it turned out that they had some. I received a series of emails checking I would be at home to sign for it in person; clearly they didn't want this stuff falling into the wrong hands. I assured them I was ready and waiting. I was eager.

And now here was the bored-looking UPS delivery guy on my doorstep with a tightly taped cardboard box, asking for a scrawl with a stylus across an electronic pad. I made my mark, closed the door and carried the box to the kitchen. Carefully I sliced through the tape with a knife. It was tightly packed with paper, in the middle of which, tied up in bubble wrap and more tape, was another package. I opened that, and pulled away the cooler pack to reveal a bright yellow tin, its top bowed out by internal pressure, as I knew it would be. The name of the manufacturer, Oskars, was in a retro '50s font across the diamond flash of red.

At last. I owned my very own tin of surströmming, or fermented Baltic herring, a food famed for its odour. Apparently it honks. Really honks. It's good at being smelly in the way Usain Bolt is good at running. One Japanese study has declared it to have the strongest intentional smell of any foodstuff on the face of the planet.

I was finally the proud owner of a tin of arguably the stinkiest delicacy on earth. I was rather excited.

The foods that most others would rather not eat have always fascinated me. I was the one early to snails and frogs' legs, the sort of dishes from which my six- and seven-year-old peers would run away gibbering. Partly this was down to opportunity. I had an affluent childhood and was raised by parents with a restaurant-going habit who encouraged my siblings and me to try whatever was on offer. I was not a fat child completely by accident. We were never warned off a food choice with a stern look and the bellowed warning 'You won't like that.' They did not take a view. It went further: we were told that we couldn't claim not to like a food unless we had tried it at least once. Because of this we tried everything. I found nothing I didn't like apart from Heinz Baked Beans. I found them to be too sweet, and I didn't like the slippery texture. Everything else was great.

Looking back, I see now that this suited me very well and not simply because I was born with an instinct for greed. The fact is, I was lousy at being a boy. I had very weak ankles and was rubbish at football. I was uncoordinated and crap at running or throwing balls or skimming pebbles. I dreaded being asked to climb trees, for fear of getting into the lowest branches and running out of strength or ambition or nerve or all three. It just wasn't part of my skill set. No matter. Instead, I could pull up at a table and dodge the business of being a boy altogether, by cutting straight to being a man. I could prove my maturity by scarfing all those foods that others my age found appalling. I may have been a little afraid of heights, but I wasn't afraid to eat snails. From time to time people have suggested to me that a liking for the sorts of foods others might spurn is an expression of machismo, a charge I have always rejected because I always felt it was down to whether I liked eating them or not. I see now that in my case they were right, or at least partly right. I used my ability to eat these foods as a way to assert a maleness that I couldn't express by other means.

As it happens, it turned out that not being able to climb trees or throw a ball wasn't much of a setback in adulthood. Now I'm a grown-up, there is no pressure to do either. Others skim pebbles across the lake. I stand by the water's edge, hands deep in pockets, and shrug. By contrast the behaviour I acquired around food as a child was a huge asset: it meant I could readily access the good stuff that so many others would still shy away from; the brilliant foods that slapped you round the chops with flavour and excitement. It was my mother who taught me, aged ten, how to eat live oysters off the half shell, with a squeeze of lemon or a drop or two of Tabasco. She took a special sort of pleasure in seeing her ten-year-old open his eyes wide at the glorious hit of iodine and brine. 'It's like eating the sea, isn't it?' she said. Then she gave me a sip of her wine, a Sancerre, which was all soft grassy notes and the high tang of cat's piss, a smell I recognized from my duties at home, cleaning out the litter tray.

I found my way quickly to calves' liver, not cooked dry and hard and bitter, as was long the style in post-war England, but soft and pink inside and with the suggestive earthiness of the intestines close to which it had sat. I quickly discovered I loved the squeak and high ureic tang of kidneys, ideally devilled, and glossy jewels of hot bone marrow from roasted bones, spread on warm sourdough with flakes of sea salt. I became obsessed with these offal experiences, enjoyed not because they really weren't so bad, but because the very farmyard smell, the whack of the duodenal, gave them power and depth. I discovered I enjoyed tripe – cow's stomach – in the Florentine style with lots of garlic and tomatoes and fiery black pepper. I wanted not just the loin of the pig, but also its feet and its snout, and best of all the gut rolled in on itself, and grilled, with mustard on the side, advertised in those bits of Britain that still remembered it as chitterlings.

Later I discovered there was a step up from chitterlings, over the water in France. I found the andouillette of Troyes, a town about ninety miles south-east of Paris, famed for its sausage using pig stomach cut into strips and scraped with a knife to remove any secretions. It is rolled in on itself and then stuffed inside the pig's large intestine, before being simmered in spiced stock. After that it can be grilled, though it does not make the slightest bit of difference to the smell, for it will always carry with it a pungency and odour that is reminiscent of the farmyard before they've cleaned it down. The pre-Second World War French prime minister Édouard Marie Herriot once said, 'Politics is like andouillette. It should smell a little like shit, but not too much,' which tells you as much about this prized sausage as it does French politics. Of course the definition of smelling 'not too much' of shit differs from person to person, because some might find any such smell more than enough. Many have recoiled from my andouillette as it has been served to me, repulsed by the stench. They look at me as though I am at best odd and at worst depraved. I enjoy this moment.

Because to me the smell they reject is the first sign of the huge pleasure to come. Andouillete does not taste as it smells, or at least not as intensely of crap as it smells. It tastes instead of a serious pigginess, with something deeper and more primeval underneath. It is the essence of animal, crossed with old sweat and fresh leather. Every time I eat one it confirms a simple truth: that the very best foods carry with them the faint whiff of death. They are a reminder of mortality, both our own and of the things we eat. Everything rots and decays in the end; this is merely dinner much further along in the process.

But then we all know this. We all know this from one of the most ubiquitous of fermented foods. We know it from cheese.

Heston Blumenthal of the Fat Duck once told me that while sitting in his office one day, then still located above the dining room, he smelled something so dense, extreme and latrine-like that he instructed his assistant to call the plumbers immediately. He simply couldn't have diners in his expensive Michelin-starred restaurant when the toilets were exploding and the whole place smelled of sweaty, unwiped arse. No need, he was told. There was nothing wrong with the toilets. The smell was the cheese trolley, which the maître d' had just put out.

Anybody who is serious about cheese will understand this. They will know that there are creations like Époisses de Bourgogne or a proper Stilton or a well-stored Brie de Meaux, one so ripe that it risks dribbling away off the table in a bid for freedom, that smell delightfully of rot and decay and, yes, shit. And yet, in the mouth rather than the nostrils, these cheeses are sublime: full of high, sour, lactic notes, and a low, dairy creaminess, and that something else we know as umami, a deep and compelling savouriness. Foods with these characteristics exist in culinary traditions from one side of the world to the other. Think of the fermented fish sauces of Thailand and Vietnam, or natto, the slippery fermented soya-bean paste of Japan; think of the stinky tofu and bean curds of Shaoxing in China, the salted anchovies of Spain, and of course my tin of surströmming. To a lesser or greater degree they all stink but taste fabulous.

The curious thing is that our sense of smell is one of our first lines of defence. It tells our brains when something dangerous might have come our way. And yet still we eat them, or at least some of us do. I am a huge fan of these foods. I think everyone should try them; that a life untouched by them is impoverished. But even I accept that a willingness to eat them in the first place is bloody odd.

In 1941 the Hungarian-born psychiatrist Dr Andras Angyal published a paper in the *Journal of Abnormal and Social Psychology* in which for the first time he defined clearly the physiological elements of disgust. It comes in many parts. We start by recoiling emotionally, but we also narrow the nostrils to stop anything getting in there. There will be 'expressive movements of the mouth region', again to stop anything gaining access, or to spit out anything that has already found its way inside. Saliva production will increase to dilute any poisons, and the throat will tighten to stop us swallowing. 'The total reaction,' Angyal said, 'is essentially a defence or protest against the penetration of the disgusting substance through the mouth and to some degree through the nostrils.' Just as the emotion of love has a purpose – to encourage us to mate so as to pass on our genes – so the emotion of disgust is designed to help keep us alive.

That said, it takes a while to manifest itself. 'While the disgust mechanism does appear to be innate, it doesn't emerge until about the age of two,' says Lucy Cooke, child psychologist and co-author of Stress Free Feeding. This is backed up by experiments conducted by Paul Rozin, Professor of Psychology at the University of Pennsylvania, and an internationally regarded expert on disgust around food. For one of his studies he lovingly crafted imitation dog faeces from peanut butter and smelly cheese. Sixty-two per cent of the children under the age of two in his study were happy to eat them. As Rozin says in his contribution to The Cambridge World History of Food, 'Below the age of about two years children seem to have little neo-phobia and, quite willingly, put almost anything into their mouths.' After that age, everything changes. As Cooke points out, 'That's the age at which toddlers can run off by themselves and pick up things that they've found and put them in their mouths. Disgust is clearly a means by which we protect ourselves.' Prior to that, Cooke adds, parents often mistake a baby's facial expressions at meeting new foods for disgust. 'Generally it's just surprise at something new.'

Choosing to fake dog poo was not just whimsy on Rozin's part. Both he and Angyal agree that faeces are, as he puts it, 'the universal disgust substance and almost certainly the first disgust, developmentally'. Which makes it all the more curious that so many of the most full-on foods do have about them the funk of excreta. It's not something that goes unacknowledged. Like superheroes, many of these hugely smelly foods have origin myths. The potent Roquefort blue cheese, for example, is said to have come about when a youth left his lunch of bread and ewe's milk cheese behind in a cave while he went off in pursuit of a pretty girl he saw in the distance. When he returned a few months later, the cheese, infected by a bacillus found in the cave, had turned into the blue-veined wonder we know today.

Similarly, all the fermented foods of the city of Shaoxing in China – the likes of stinky tofu, fermented amaranth stalks, or mouldy 'thousand sheets' bean curd – have a single story. As described by the Chinese food expert and writer Fuchsia Dunlop, in a paper delivered to the Oxford Food Symposium in 2010, the legend tells of the Yue king Gou Jian being enslaved by the neighbouring state of Wu. The Wu king fell ill with an unknown illness. Gou Jian was asked for his advice, and predicted the king's imminent recovery after tasting Gou Jian's excrement, a neat trick if you can pull it off. The Wu king did indeed recover and in his gratitude freed Gou Jian, but the manner by which he had gained his release was seen by his people as a massive humiliation. After all he had secured it by eating another man's shit. As a result it was decreed that the people of Yue should henceforth eat their rice with 'stinking foods'. The legend makes an explicit, almost celebratory link between these foods and faeces. To be fair, even Dunlop describes the smell of some of them as 'horrifying', and she's a fan.

You do not have to be an anthropologist to spot that these delicacies became a part of our diet out of necessity. When resources are scarce you cannot afford to throw away either the intestine of the pig or the stalks of the amaranth plant, and you need to find a way to preserve them. If the raw materials are plentiful you can salt them, but if they're not, you can use only small amounts with water, which results in fermentation, the production of bacteria which have the effect of preserving a certain amount of the food's nutritional value. What's more intriguing is why those of us no longer driven by the imperative of poverty should still want to eat them.

Rozin attributes that partly to what he calls the human instinct to 'benign masochism'. Just as we enjoy being scared by horror movies, or being made to feel sad by weepies, we will eat things that don't at first glance seem pleasurable. As Rozin says, humans are unique in the mammalian world 'in developing strong likes for foods that are innately unpalatable'. The first time a child tastes alcohol is rarely a pleasant experience. It can be bitter and burn the back of your throat. You have to push on through with booze to recognize it has its own rewards. Most obviously, enormous numbers of us enjoy the burn of chilli, and we are rewarded for those efforts by a dose of endorphins, the natural opiate-like substances that the body releases to deal with pain.

But the key is this: all of these foods really do taste so very much better than they smell. Famously, the durian fruit of South East Asia – known locally as the king of fruits – has a stench that is said to resemble either rotting flesh or raw sewage (but of course). It's banned from much public transport, the prohibition indicated by an image of the fruit inside a red circle with a slash through it, exactly as is used for cigarettes. And yet it tastes delicious, and is eaten both fresh and as a flavouring for biscuits, cakes, drinks and even soups. Likewise, andouillette really does not taste of the uncleaned farmyard, however much it might smell of it. The strange thing about this is that it is our sense of smell which accounts for anywhere from 75 per cent to 95 per cent of the taste of our food. When we lose our sense of taste during a heavy cold, the virus doesn't affect our tastebuds but our sense of smell, as the mucous membrane inside our nostrils becomes inflamed and our nose becomes blocked. Without it we are lost.

Which means something rather odd: that how we smell things is different inside the body than outside. As Rozin has said, smell is the only one of the senses used not just to experience and explore the outside world, but also the internal. 'There is definitely a difference,' says Professor Peter Barham of Bristol University, who has long investigated the science of our food. 'As a result of MRI technology we now know that different parts of the brain light up depending upon whether you are breathing in or breathing out.' What that actually means we know far less about, but I can't pretend I'm not grateful. Because it means I have access to a whole bunch of food experiences that might otherwise be closed to me.

In many ways, I know I have stacked up the evidence for the prosecution against me. I have all but made the case that my proclaimed love for the stinkiest of foods is in some way bogus. I have admitted to an element of machismo, founded in a misshapen childhood in which I was trying to locate a way to achieve adulthood, and did so through foods others reject. I have admitted that I might be enjoying them at least partly out of benign masochism, a desire to do something that on the face of it smells like it might hurt me. I'm willing to go even further. In a paper for the *Journal of Folklore Research*, published in 2000, Michael Owen Jones argued that the very awfulness might be a big part of the attraction. 'To indulge in the disgusting,' he wrote, 'is to be tempted by the forbidden.' And we all know how very tempting the forbidden can be.

And yet, even while acknowledging all of this as part of the weft and weave of my behaviour, I still insist that I love the stinkiest of foods because they are the most delicious; that I cannot imagine a life without cheeses smelling densely of the latrines, without offals embossed with the aromas of the slaughterhouse, without the products of fermentation that have given us the most pungent of fish sauces. The stinky is its own reward, and we should all be open to it. It's what both life and a little bit of death are about.

One windy winter's morning I took my tin of surströmming up to my local park. There is a story about a German landlord who, in 1981, was taken to court for evicting a tenant who had sprayed surströmming liquor all over the shared stairwell of his building. The landlord won his case by opening a can inside the court-room. The court ruled that it 'had convinced itself that the disgusting smell of the fish brine far exceeded the degree that fellow-tenants in the building could be expected to tolerate'. If the stuff really did smell as badly as all that, I wasn't going to risk opening it in the back garden. The stench of fermenting fish might just push my neighbours over the edge.

I prepared for the outing very carefully. I had a plastic plate, a sharp knife, a fork, a lot of kitchen roll, a tin opener, a bunch of plastic bags and a sense of adventure. Up by a copse, with the wind pulling at my ludicrous hair, I slowly opened the tin. The first whiff was nothing much: just the sour smell of a storage space long used for fish. But as I worked the blade of the can opener round the edge the smell really expanded. I felt my face pulling involuntarily into the universal expression of disgust as described by Dr Andras Angyal in 1941: my nose wrinkled to close my nostrils, my lips puckered, my mouth went into overdrive on saliva production to dilute any toxins. Yes, the smell was faecal. But there was also decay and then the higher, punchier notes of festering sea life. When my children were babies we used scented plastic bags to dispose of their soiled nappies. These would then go into a kind of vacuum pack bin. Once it was full, usually after a few days, you emptied all the nappies. The smell would be weird and horrifying but also strangely intimate: old shit and piss, but all overlaid by a sickly sweetness from decaying industrial perfume. In time I came to associate this smell with my babies and because, as a young parent, I had a pathological love for them, there was something oddly comforting and beguiling about it. The stench was the reality of parenthood.

Surströmming smells a bit like that, though very much

amplified. It is armpits and sweat and death and decay and wrongness. I could well see how some people would recoil from this and refuse to go any further.

Ah, but I am experienced in the way of the stinky. I know that these things generally taste much better than they smell. Admittedly, this wouldn't be hard. For all that smell of rot, the herring inside retain both their shape and glossy, silvery sheen. I plucked one out with a fork, and cut through the very soft flesh, pulling it away from the intact spine. I considered it for a moment, then dropped it into my mouth and looked away from the can, as if I didn't want the surströmming to see what I was up to. No, it did not taste as it smelled, or at least not quite. It was salty, but it was also very savoury indeed. It reminded me of salted anchovies but with the volume turned up to fifteen, or of a Thai curry made with fermented fish guts that I ate once. In one way it was appalling, but it was also hugely compelling. In Sweden it tends to be eaten rolled inside flatbread with slices of new potato, onions and soured cream, and I could see exactly how it would work partnered with these more mellow ingredients.

More important, I think, is that Swedes attach ritual to its eating. It's not just something they have at the back of the fridge and get out when they fancy some surströmming for their tea. Friends are invited round. The ingredients are laid out. Attention is paid to the opening of the tin. Alcohol is drunk. In that context the smell becomes a proof of who they are. They wouldn't want it to smell any other way, because if it did it wouldn't be surströmming, and that's what they're here for. It's the taste of something that died long ago, magically kept from falling over the edge into oblivion.

And that's the point with all these stinky foods, these ingredients that carry with them that faint whiff of death. Like jumping into an ice-cold river, the experience is utterly invigorating. The food may be more dead than most, but by eating it you can't avoid the thought that you are very much more alive. And who wouldn't want to be reminded of that?

ANDOUILLETTE GRATIN

Outside of France it's probably easiest to get hold of andouillette online. Look for those with the AAAAA rating, which means the producer has been approved by the Association Amicale des Amateurs d'Andouillette Authentique (literally the Friendly Club of Lovers of Authentic Andouillette), an organization set up by a bunch of enthusiasts in the 1970s. At the time of writing only eight producers have the rating. True andouillette lovers will tell you that they should simply be eaten grilled with a bit of mustard on the side. But for those who find that a little intimidating, there is this andouillette gratin, my version of the Lyonnais classic. Yes, it's rich. What do you bloody expect? It's from Lyon.

Serves 4 as a hefty starter

500g waxy new potatoes
2 medium-sized onions
olive oil
butter
1 clove of garlic, crushed
275ml chicken stock (the real thing is great, but from a
    cube is fine)
125ml double cream
3 tbsp grain mustard
sea salt and ground black pepper
250g andouillette (probably about 2 whole sausages)
80g breadcrumbs

- Boil the potatoes, skin on, until cooked but not falling apart. Drain and leave to cool.
- Meanwhile, slice the onions and sauté gently in a little olive oil. After 5 minutes, add a knob of butter and the garlic. When the onions are soft and translucent, leave to cool.

- Heat the oven to 220°C/425°F/gas 7.
- While waiting for the potatoes and onions to cool, heat the stock in a pan. Set to a gentle simmer, then add the cream. Gently reduce until it begins to thicken and can coat the back of a spoon. Stir in the mustard. Add a good pinch of sea salt and a grind of black pepper.
- Roughly chop the andouillette and the potatoes and place in a large bowl.
- Add the onions and garlic to the bowl and mix well. Add the sauce and mix again. Add another good pinch of sea salt and a grind of black pepper. Remember, there are quite a lot of potatoes in there that need seasoning.
- There's enough here for four oval oven dishes measuring 20cm by 15cm, but you'll have your own dishes to cook this in. It could be cooked in one large oven dish, and portioned out, as long as it isn't piled in to a depth of much more than 4cm.
- Top with the breadcrumbs, and dot with knobs of butter.
- Cook in the oven for about 15 minutes, or until the breadcrumbs are golden brown. The full farmyard smell is likely to be released during the cooking process.
- Serve to friends who are not namby-pamby about their food, and understand that the really good stuff smells like this.

9.

Thou shalt not mistake food for pharmaceuticals

Superfoods. To get the most out of them you don't need the will-power to stick with an unappetizing diet of kale and something that smells like ground-down compost. You don't even need an understanding of nutrition. What you really need is fully function-ing eyesight, because that will enable you to read the small print on the side of the packs. That, in turn, means you'll be able to have a right old laugh, an opportunity you will not want to miss given that laughter really is the only definable health benefit those super-foods are likely to gift you. We do at least know that laughter is great for reducing stress, and that genuinely is good for your health.

Take Berry Green SuperFood, a supplement powder produced by Amazing Grass, a company founded in Kansas in 2002, and now operating out of Newport Beach, California. As the name of the company suggests, the product smells of grass clippings and des-peration. The packaging hasn't met a buzzword it didn't like. It offers 'alkalizing and energizing plant-based nutrition'. It contains both goji and acai berries, the supermodels of the superfood world, said to be high in mysteriously wonderful antioxidants. It is also 'vegan & gluten free'. Thank God for that. I like vegans but I couldn't eat a whole one.

A 480g pot, enough for 60 servings to be mixed up as a drink or thrown into soups, currently costs £21.33 via amazon.co.uk. So what does that money get you? Well, apparently it 'supports over-all health and wellness' and 'healthy immune and detoxification functions'. It also 'includes a probiotic and enzyme blend to support digestive health'. Wow. Sounds great. But hang on. Squint slightly and you'll see there's a tiny asterisk at the end of each of these terrific claims which directs you to another, down at the bottom of the label, in even smaller print: 'These statements have not been evaluated by the Food and Drug Administration. This product is not intended to diagnose, treat, cure or prevent any disease.' In short, they have no proof of anything they've said. None at all. But it all sounds nice, doesn't it?

Here's another one, a packet of Organic Raw Goji Berries, packed in north London by a company called Inspiral. It doesn't use the word 'superfood' on its packaging, but it does on its website. It says a lot of things on its website (which we'll come to), though clearly it would love to say more. As the label says, 'Due to EU rules we can't share all of our nutritional research on these foods with you. Search online for health benefits.' And what are these irritating EU rules restricting our access to the glorious information that Inspiral has but can't share? They're the rules prohibiting the publication of health claims for food products unless they have been properly tested and verified using recognized scientific methodology. The tests can be as basic as proving that the products contain the substances the manufacturers claim are in there.

No matter. As Inspiral knows full well, it's not a major problem that superfood producers can't verify the claims they'd like to make for their food products, because swathes of the media are happy to do the marketing job for them. Seemingly reputable journalists will confidently tell you that cabbage contains substances proven to have 'cancer-fighting properties'. They'll tell you that chia seeds reduce the risk of heart disease; that blueberries can reduce the hardening of arteries and therefore the risk of heart attack and stroke. Apparently beetroot can help prevent dementia. Wheatgrass can boost red blood cell production. Both chocolate and broccoli can prevent high blood pressure, cardiovascular disease and cancer. Good old chocolate and broccoli. There are similar claims for pomegranate juice and kale, goji berries and green tea, oily fish and garlic. Forget going to the doctor. Stop wasting your money at the chemist's. Your local branch of Whole Foods Market has all the pharmaceuticals you could ever need. It's your dinner that will stop you from dying.

This, of course, is true. Your dinner is important in keeping you alive, as is your breakfast and lunch. Food is vital to human health. Personally, I'm addicted to it. If I don't get at least two (and preferably three) fixes of food a day, I develop symptoms of withdrawal. It's called being hungry. A varied diet, high in fruit and vegetables, with a good amount of fibre, and a reasonable balance of carbs to protein, will do a superb job of keeping me alive and healthy. But there are no foods that behave like pharmaceuticals. Not a single one. The salad as magic health bullet does not exist.

The bizarre thing is that the medical establishment keeps saying this. It keeps banging on about it. Cancer Research UK dismisses the term 'superfood' as nothing more than a marketing gimmick. 'There is not one food that will sort you out cancer-wise,' says Sarah Williams, Cancer UK's health information manager. 'There really is not one thing that will make a difference.' Rick Wilson, Director of Dietetics and Nutrition at King's College Hospital in south London until his recent retirement, is infuriated by it. 'The term "superfood" drives me nuts. We don't eat foods. We eat a diet. The whole idea of marketing, say, kale as a universal panacea is ridiculous.'

To the intense frustration of many of those scientifically qualified people, a big part of the problem lies with truly appalling science. Because not all scientific studies are equal. Some have poor methodology. Perhaps they don't involve a big enough sample of people, or there isn't a control group. Others aren't examining what you're told they're examining. A study will look at the effect of a compound found in a food – lycopene, for example, which gives tomatoes their red colour, or glucosinolates in cabbage – but only in a concentrated, isolated form and only in the laboratory. A study might find that one of these compounds has an impact on cancer cells in the lab environment. Suddenly we're being told the foodstuff containing it has cancer-fighting properties. However, that particular study tells you nothing about how those compounds impact on the human body when eaten as part of a food, or in combination with other foods. You cannot extrapolate from what happened in the lab. All you can say is that something interesting was seen, and that it may be worth investigating further.

'We are regularly funding research into compounds found in foods,' says Sarah Williams, 'but that tells you nothing about the foods they come from. For example, aspirin comes from the bark of a particular willow tree, but no one would tell you to go lick a willow tree to treat your headache.' Tim Spector, Professor of Genetic Epidemiology at King's College London, and author of *The Diet Myth*, finds it all very frustrating. He decided to examine claims made for coconut oil, a fat which has been celebrated as a cure-all for everything from cancer through heart disease to obesity. 'I looked up the studies,' Professor Spector says. 'Some were plainly bogus in that they didn't exist, and others claimed to be published in journals that I could find no evidence of. I couldn't find a single serious study on coconut oil. And yet if you go on the Web it's praised to the stars.'

Indeed it is. Take the website authoritynutrition.com, which proclaims an evidence-based approach. Or, as it puts it, 'Everything we say is based on scientific evidence, and written by experts . . . Our main goal is to write the best nutrition articles on the Internet.' It sounds reassuring, doesn't it? It sounds exactly like the sort of thing a cynical man like me, hungry for scientific proof of the health benefits of foodstuffs, should crave. And the website does indeed have an article entitled '10 proven health benefits of coconut oil'. These include the news that coconut oil contains a unique combination of fatty acids with 'proven' – that word again – medicinal properties, that eating it can help you burn fat, that populations who eat loads of coconut are seriously healthy, and so on. Each claim comes with a hyperlink to a source.

And so, in an attempt to find the proof the website says it has, I start clicking away.

The first link takes me to an article on the very same website about saturated fats. The second link, about fats called medium-chain triglycerides, goes to an article on Wikipedia, as does the third, an article about some Pacific islanders who eat a lot of coconut. Wikipedia can be a useful quick reference, as long as you are aware it also contains a lot of unverified information which is utter cobblers. Certainly it's not a reliable source of scientific information. There are a number of links to purely lab-based studies of compounds found in coconut oil, but which were not extracted from coconut for those studies; and a bunch about the impact of certain diets, which can be achieved without eating coconut oil and which, in any case, are controversial. There are links to studies on the impact of a diet (again, not specifically mentioning coconut oil) on Alzheimer's, which even they admit is speculation, and one with a title that doesn't even read as English. It's called 'Ketogenicity of soybean oil, coconut oil and their respective fatty acids for the chick', and while it says the full text is available, there is none.

There are just two links to papers that specifically examine the properties of coconut oil, both looking at its impact on weight loss. One was a study of an extremely small sample of obese women. There were just forty of them, with only half of them on the coconut oil and the other half on soya-bean oil. It shows that both displayed a reduction in body mass index, with the coconut-oil group also showing a very small extra reduction in waist measurement. But the sample really is so tiny as to make it impossible to have confidence in any conclusions. The other paper was on an even smaller sample, and had no control group, so is even less convincing. Other than that there is the suggestion that it's nice for your skin and hair, though as it happens many things are. And coconut oil will, of course, make you smell of coconut.

Authoritynutrition.com is not trying to deceive anyone. It may indeed be achieving its goal of posting the best nutrition articles on the Net, because God knows there's an awful lot of crap out there. It just seems that its grasp of what equates to proper scientific proof is tenuous. The fact is that the world is a desperately complicated place, and yet we crave simplicity. As a result we will see it wherever we can.

For example, the one thing we are told we can believe is that there's something called antioxidants – present in a lot of fruit and green vegetables – and that they are Good, with a capital G. We are told they have 'cancer-protecting properties'. Those are my quote marks, but put the words 'antioxidant cancer prevention' into Google and you'll get 1.45 million results. We understand them as good because they fight free radicals. These free radicals are Bad with a capital B, because they are unstable elements that come off any chemical reaction in the body using oxygen. They in turn can cause oxidative stress, which might do damage, say, to your DNA, and hence be involved in the processes leading to cancer. If antioxidants fight free radicals, that has to be a good thing, right? Not necessarily, because free radicals also destroy invading bacteria and are vital in other bodily processes.

As Duane Mellor, a spokesperson for the British Dietetic Association, explained to the journalist Dara Mohammadi in the *Guardian* in 2015, the most common antioxidants circulating in our bodies 'are the ones we make ourselves – glutathione and uric acid – followed by vitamins A, C and E, which we get from normal food anyway. Many of the antioxidants in things like chia seeds are there to stop the plant oils going rancid, or to protect them from sunlight damage, and may not be that available to our bodies anyway. So although the EFSA [European Food Safety Authority] allows manufacturers to claim that their products are rich in antioxidants – because they are – manufacturers are not allowed to claim any health benefits.' What's more, a variety of studies into antioxidants taken as supplements have found little or no evidence that they are advantageous to our health.

It's discouraging isn't it, the way the evidence refuses to line up with our hopes. Still, we can all dream, which is exactly what Inspiral, the company that sold me those goji berries, does. As its packaging told me, the company can't make claims for its products. But on its website it can tell you what the scientists are looking at right now. So one of its products is made with barley-grass and wheatgrass, both of which contain chlorophyll, which in turn contains an antioxidant enzyme which is currently 'being researched for its anti-ageing and tissue-replenishing properties'. There's parsley leaf, which apparently contains flavonoids, which are being researched for their 'roles in cancer prevention and immune system modulation'. And on and on it goes. All this stuff is being looked at. It's being researched. It's being considered. Surely that's a good enough reason to buy the stuff?

The problem is that just because a substance found in a food is being studied to see if it has any interesting properties, doesn't mean that it actually does.

For example, I am currently being studied to see if I can fly by waving my arms up and down, which, I'm sure you'll agree, is very exciting indeed.

Oh dear, it turns out I can't fly.

What a disappointment.

There is one other approach to the whole business of super-foods and science, and that is simply to get things wrong. The most famous example of this is the self-styled 'nutritionist' Gillian McKeith, who had a show on British television in the early noughties in which she called herself a doctor, on account of a PhD she had bought from a non-accredited university in the United States. She declared that we should eat more green vegetables because they contain large amounts of chlorophyll, which would oxygenate our blood. Put aside the fact that there are no lungs in our intestines and hence no way for any oxygen in there to get into our bloodstream. As any schoolchild knows, chlorophyll produces oxygen as a result of sunshine. Your guts are one place where there is definitely none of that. McKeith was famously discredited over this claim years ago, and forced by the UK's advertising authorities to stop calling herself a doctor.

But in the world of food as pharmaceutical, this kind of thing is still very common.

Take the website of Primrose's Kitchen, a superfood company based in Dorset and run by Primrose Matheson, who trained as a naturopath at something called the College for Naturopathic Medicine in London. A blog post on the treatment of thrush included the advice to stick a garlic clove inside your vagina at night, and announced that 'antibiotics kill every bacteria they come across', which is simply not true. We have lots of different antibiotics precisely because they each kill off different bugs (until you get to the very rarely used broad-spectrum antibiotics). Still, it's okay for Matheson to say things like this, because her website carries a disclaimer. It says, 'The articles written in the blogs and website are the opinions of the authors. Primrose's Kitchen and its contributors make no claims in what they say ... Primrose's Kitchen takes no responsibility for customers choosing to treat themselves. Your use of this information is at your own risk.' As ever, when it comes to superfoods, you always need to pay attention to the small print.

I spoke to Matheson by phone. I asked her if the disclaimer meant that she acknowledged everything that she said was not worth the digital ink spilled to say it. She told me that it was something her web designer had put there and that, in any case, 'You are your own teacher. I don't believe in taking anything as gospel, including my own writings.' But the inaccuracies in what you're saying about antibiotics, I told her, aren't just a matter of opinion. They're a fact.

'Oh,' she said. 'I don't believe in facts.'

There didn't seem much point in continuing the conversation. I said goodbye.

According to the late William Safire, the political essayist who wrote a column on the origins of words for *The New York Times*, the term 'superfood' was first used in an article in the Jamaican newspaper the *Daily Gleaner* in 1915. The foodstuff being described was wine, which makes sense to me. I think wine is super too. I'd go so far as to call it terrific. A couple of years later the United Fruit Company began an aggressive advertising campaign bigging up the specific health virtues of bananas, making the kind of claims for them which would have been recognized by today's superfood aficionados.

Intriguingly, these two moments sit right in the middle of the growth and expansion of the modern pharmaceutical industry. From the 1880s onwards, both research into, and the development of, therapies for the likes of asthma and diabetes had accelerated. Barbiturates were developed alongside anti-infective drugs, culminating, in 1928, with Alexander Fleming's discovery of penicillin, eventually mass produced after the Second World War to dramatic effect. It is not overstating these advances to describe them as a revolution in medical practice. The age of drug therapy had arrived. And as with all revolutions it replaced something. That something was food.

Hippocrates of Kos, the Greek physician of the fifth century BC, famously insisted that each of us should 'let food be thy medicine', not least because there was little else in the way of treatments. Much of the history of the first two millennia of treating the sick involves varying theories on which foods do what. As the Roman encyclopaedist Celsus wrote in the first century BC, 'It is clear that each man follows his own ideas rather than what he has found to be true by actual fact.' By the eighteenth century, however, British hospitals had established that good general nutrition was a significant part of helping the sick to recover. Hence the full standard hospital diet was a formidable thing: it included half a pound of beef or mutton, served four times a week, alongside a whole loaf of bread and four pints of beer daily (probably less alcoholic than the beer we're used to today, though enough to keep the patients permanently and rather happily pissed). It's worth noting that when the United States Food, Drug and Cosmetic Act passed into law in June 1938, it included no clear differentiation between what was considered food and what was considered a drug.

My late mother trained as a nurse in the 1940s and was taught the importance of what was then called 'invalid foods': calves' foot jellies, beef teas and the like, which helped those who had been seriously ill to train their stomachs to accept food again. Towards the end of her life, she was in intensive care for more than a month and, as she embarked on the long road to recovery, was infuriated that all this training in the importance of nutrition appeared to have been forgotten completely. Anybody who has followed the debate about the collapsing quality of British hospital food in the post-war era – and especially after the Thatcher government introduced a market principle to feeding the acutely sick in the 1980s – will recognize the arguments: that pharmaceuticals can't do everything, and that good diet has to be a part of the healing process.

Rick Wilson, reflecting on his time at King's College Hospital, one of the largest teaching hospitals in London, has much sympathy with the argument that the drug revolution stunted medical interest in nutrition. 'One hundred and fifty years ago, diet and pharmaceuticals were one and the same thing,' he says. 'There is a sense in which we threw the baby out with the bathwater. The annual food bill at King's is around £3 million or £4 million. The pharmaceutical bill is between £70 million and £80 million, and an awful lot of those drugs are used to treat the impact of nutrition issues, be it malnutrition in the elderly, diabetes or cardiovascular issues.' The problem, he says, is that doctors have very poor training in the subject. British medical training takes five years, but only a few days of that are dedicated to the impact of diet. 'And it's not something they are examined on.'

This has left a gaping hole in the market, opening the way for the rise of the bogus science of superfoods, or what have been dubbed, irritatingly, nutraceuticals, which is the sort of mangling of the language that makes me want to punch people. I ask Sarah Williams of Cancer Research UK why she thinks her overall message – that there are no individual foodstuffs that will treat your diseases or make you smarter or protect you from cancer; that what matters is a balanced diet – has failed to gain purchase. She says, 'I think it's because what I'm saying is not very sexy. Telling people to eat a good, balanced diet is rather boring and not even that sciency. Whereas the stuff on the Web that's then republished by the media has appropriated the language of science.' It talks about studies and subjects. These food studies are published to look like pukka studies, even though they aren't. As Professor Tim Spector says, 'The media just loves it, so if a journalist comes across some story about a food protecting you from cancer, they're pretty much guaranteed a front-page slot for any old drivel.' To be fair, he says, it's not always the fault of the journalist. 'They're under increasing pressure to write story after story.'

Hence any old guff can find its way into print. Of course, in this the academic institutions really are culpable. This is because all universities need to prove their worth, and one way to do so is to get newspaper headlines proving that they are a centre of exciting research. For example, not long ago I received a press release from Queen Margaret University in Edinburgh, a highly reputable seat of learning with centres of excellence in a variety of disciplines, including food and nutrition. It had secured funding to examine the benefits of a brand of confectionery called IQ Superfood Chocolate. According to the breathless press release, the first finding was that it contained a higher level of antioxidants compared to other leading brands, which as we know does not actually mean it's healthier for you in any way.

The other claim, however, was remarkable. Its research had shown that the chocolate 'has the potential to increase the reaction times of Scotland's toughest rugby players'. Apparently it improved cognitive function, accuracy and speed.

Say what? There's a chocolate you can eat to make you a better sportsman? Rather than a big fat, lardy couch potato? What very heaven is this?

And then I started reading the research. The study involved just a dozen blokes, which is a statistically tiny sample. And there was no mention of a control group, i.e. no group of people who either weren't fed the IQ Superfood Chocolate or were fed no chocolate at all, so you could check that the results weren't a fluke. Hilariously, the press release described this as 'robust scientific analysis'. But then it would say that, because it is a university looking for headlines. I read to the end of the press release, looking for a reference to a peer-reviewed academic journal where I could study the findings in full. There was none.

I managed to track down one of the lead researchers on the study, a PhD student called Suzanne Zaremba. She confirmed there was no control group. 'This was just a small unpublished pilot study.' Unpublished? You mean your findings never underwent any form of peer review, the process by which academics verify each other's work? 'No. I do appreciate it was by no means rigorous, hence it wasn't written up.' Except in a press release aimed at bigging up the university in a bunch of headlines, one of which it secured in the *Herald*, one of Scotland's leading newspapers. I asked Zaremba what she thought of the term 'superfood'. She sighed. 'There is no such a thing as a superfood.'

Well, quite. I ordered a few bars, the plush peppermint at £2.50 a bar. It's rather nice chocolate, as it happens, bitter but refreshing. Eating it did not improve my piano playing. Oh, how I wish there was a food that would do that. Oh well. It's back to the practising.

The world has always been full of hucksters and fakes, turning a dime on false promises and showmanship. And there has always been an audience for those hucksters and fakes. Humanity has an innate tendency to sweet hopefulness. What separates out the superfood movement is the fact that the vast majority of those flogging the stuff believe what they're saying too, and the movement around them seems to be growing both noisier and more insistent.

Why should this be? Partly, I suspect it's a response to millennial fears around climate change and damage to the environment in general. Humanity seems intent on poisoning its habitat, so people are looking to find ways to avoid poisoning themselves. They talk about eating foods to detoxify themselves, even though there is no food which will detoxify you and nor do you need them. If you have a liver and kidneys, your body is already doing the job for you. In a world seemingly full of poisons and carcinogens there is a panic and fear; a mad desire to avoid being contaminated. Hence there is a belief that certain foods will boost your immune system, even though if your immune system really was boosted it would be a terrible thing. Your immune system fights anything alien to your body, by flushing it out through the production of snot, or cooking it to death by giving you a fever. If your immune system became boosted, you would be running a constant temperature in response to things that weren't a threat. Eventually you'd develop an autoimmune disease as your boosted immune system started going to war on your own body.

Oh, but look. I've gone all sciency again, which is just plain annoying. So let's go for one last bit of quack psychology. People want to believe in foods as pharmaceuticals because, in an extremely complex world, it gives them the illusion that they are back in control, despite the fact that these foods do nothing and are a waste of money.

You know the deal: eat a good, balanced diet, take exercise, don't stress the small stuff, and keep your fingers crossed that you win the genetic lottery. That's advice you can have for free. You're welcome.

The following recipes will not cure you of cancer. They will not make you smarter or boost your immune system. But they are killer salads, which are both delicious and will make you feel like you're being kind to yourself.

CUCUMBER SALAD, TWO WAYS

The brilliance of this simple salad is that a change in the accessories and seasonings completely shifts the basic version geographically, from Eastern Europe to Asia.

Serves 4 as a side, or 2 greedy people

2 cucumbers
100ml rapeseed oil, or other clean-tasting vegetable oil
50ml white wine vinegar
1tsp sea salt

For the Eastern European version

2 tbsp chopped fresh dill
1 tsp caster sugar

For the Asian version

2 red chillies, finely sliced
2–3 cloves of garlic, crushed with the flat blade of a knife, then chopped
a bunch of fresh coriander, torn rather than chopped
1 tbsp sesame oil

- Use a peeler to remove the cucumber skin. Slice each one in half along its length, then scrape out the seeds with a teaspoon. Slice in half again lengthways and chop into 0.5cm pieces. Place in a large bowl.
- Mix the oil and vinegar together in a small bowl. Pour over the cucumbers, add the sea salt and stir. Add more salt if you think it can take it.
- Give it a couple of hours in the fridge before serving.
- The salad is great as it is, but if you do want to move it on, add the chopped dill and sugar to turn it into the kind of cucumber salad found across swathes of Eastern

Europe. Alternatively, head even further east by adding the combo of chillies, garlic, coriander and sesame oil.

PEPPER SALAD

This salad is a victory of slicing. If you like Zen tasks in the kitchen, this is definitely for you. It seems like a lot of vegetables, but frankly it's not worth making less and it will all get eaten. Likewise, it sounds like a lot of dressing, but the entire salad has to sink into it. By the time it has relaxed, it will probably be at least two-thirds of the volume you started with.

Serves 8

6 bell peppers of mixed colours
2 medium-sized red onions (though white will do)
a couple of dozen black olives, stoned
a bunch of fresh basil
2 cloves of garlic, crushed

For the dressing

approx. 250ml olive oil
approx. 125ml white wine vinegar
2 tsp flaky sea salt
a good grind of black pepper
1 tsp caster sugar

- Remove the top of each pepper and deseed, then slice each one in half vertically. Now slice into very fine strips. You'll find this easier if you make an incision at the top and bottom of each half so you can press them flat on to your board. Also slice them with the inside facing up, rather than the glossy outside, which even the sharpest blade can have problems with.

- Cut the onions in half and then slice them finely. Chop up the black olives and tear up the basil leaves.
- Put it all into a large bowl, ideally one that's wide rather than deep. Add the garlic and mix everything together.
- In a separate bowl, mix the oil with the vinegar in a ratio of two to one. It's difficult to know exactly how much you will need because of the variable size of your peppers and the bowl you've put them in, but the dressing should come up to about 8cm below the surface of the salad.
- Add the sea salt, black pepper and sugar to the dressing, mix well, pour it over the salad and give it a good stir. Place in the fridge for an hour. Stir it again. The mixture will have sunk, and will continue to do so. Leave it in the fridge for at least another 2 hours, returning to it every hour to give it a stir.

10.

Honour thy pig

We end as we began, with David Cameron. This time, however, things are reversed. At the start of the first commandment – the instruction to eat with your hands wherever possible – the pork product was going into the British prime minister. It was a hot dog eaten, shamefully, with a knife and fork. Now a bit of the British prime minister is going into the pork product. Or at least that's the allegation: that, during an event held in the 1980s by the Piers Gaveston Society, a self-consciously decadent Oxford University dining club named after Edward II's lover, the young Cameron shoved his penis into the mouth of a dead pig.

Look, we've all been there.

The source of the story, an unnamed Oxford contemporary and fellow MP, refused to break cover during the feverish speculation that attended its publication in September 2015. Michael Ashcroft, the billionaire peer, former Tory party treasurer and donor to the party, had co-written and funded the biography of Cameron in which the story appeared, and certainly had an axe to grind: he believed he would be given a senior ministerial post when the Conservatives came to power in 2010 in return for all his dosh, and was furious that he had not. Later Isabel Oakeshott, former political editor of the *Sunday Times* and his co-author, admitted the source might have been 'slightly deranged' and that the whole story was just a throwaway anecdote.

Far more interesting than the 'did he, didn't he?' – sorry to be a killjoy, but let's go with 'probably didn't' – is the potency of the image. It just had to be a pig. Nothing else would have had the impact or significance. Nothing else would have been as deviant. In the raucous myths and legends surrounding these things, sexual congress with a sheep has always been for the utterly desperate; with a horse or cow, for the deluded and overly ambitious. But a pig! They are the farmyard animals that have always lived closest to us. Their physiology is so similar to ours that their heart valves and their insulin keep some of us alive. It is the bestial line that looks far too easy to cross. It was no accident that George Orwell chose the pigs to be the dominant personalities in his novel *Animal Farm*, so that, by the end of the story, the rest of the farmyard could look 'from pig to man, and from man to pig' and find that 'already it was impossible to say which was which'.

Perhaps because of that intimacy, they have also been the subject of more taboos than any other animals. Whole cultures define themselves by their refusal to have anything to do with them. The Muslim stand-up comedian Aatif Nawaz has mined endless material out of his mother's inability to even say the word 'pig'. In the first episode of Charlie Brooker's darkly satirical comedy series *Black Mirror*, broadcast on British TV in 2011, the denouement involved the demand that the fictional prime minister should have congress with a pig on live TV so as to secure the release of a kidnapped member of the royal family. With that in mind, the Ashcroft allegation ends up looking like overcooked fiction imitating art.

These cultural sensitivities obviously make pigs extremely interesting. But all of that trails far behind one particular quality of the pig in terms of importance, the major consideration for a man like me: the fact that they are just so utterly edible. I am powerless in the face of roast pork belly – the way the crunch of the crackling gives way to the soft, hot fat just dissolving to liquid beneath and then the sweet fibrous meat below that. I adore spare ribs, whether glazed or not, and chops and hams. And bacon is one of those foodstuffs which gives pause to even a die-hard atheist like me: is it too much to wonder whether some higher power was at work when evolution brought forth these animals, which were just waiting to be dry-cured and sliced and fried and slapped between two pieces of bread to make the single greatest sandwich known to humanity?

Oh, shut up and get frying.

In culinary terms there is quite simply no animal like the pig. The joke is that you can eat everything but the squeak. Or, as historian Dr Annie Gray once told me when I interviewed her for a BBC radio documentary investigating the enduring appeal of piggery, 'The only thing you can't eat is the poo inside the intestines, but you can probably feed it back to other pigs.'

From the head, both the snout and the ears are prized as crisped or jellied items in culinary traditions from Europe to Asia. The lozenges of meat in the cheeks can be long-braised, as indeed can the whole head, then spiced and pressed to make brawn. There is pig tongue, which can be simmered and cooled and served in slices with a punchy sauce gribiche.

Obviously there are the standard cuts, the loins and the chops, the ribs and the belly, the legs for hams – both fresh and long-cured, as per the Italian and Spanish traditions – and the shoulders for slow smoking to make pulled pork. For without pulled pork what would hipster American barbecue joints in Nuneaton have to serve? On the outside, the skin makes perfect scratchings, and its high protein content can be used to boost the nutritional value of cheap sausages. Deep inside there is the offal, prized in culinary traditions across the world, from Mexico, where tripe turns up in a fabulous stew called menudo, with the thrilling tang of the duodenal, to the liver-and-lung-rich faggots of South Wales, or the funky, powerful dishes of Sichuan in China, which loves frying up those inner organs with fistfuls of red chilli and peppercorns. Pig kidneys and spleens can be grilled. The intestines can be used as sausage casings, and the blood gathered up at the animal's slaughter can be turned into black pudding, boudin noir or morcilla, depending on what country you happen to call home. The Chinese will eat wobbly cubes of pig blood in soup. In passing I mention andouillette once again, because I must. Stop flinching at the back there. Remember the mantra: if you're going to bang an animal on the head for food, you have a moral responsibility to eat as much of it as you can. The pig is by far the most obliging in that department. The fat is brilliant in pastry, or as a medium for food preservation, or smeared across my face, all hot and slippery. The trotters and tail can be braised and either fried as they are, or boned out, stuffed and simmered again. Any bit of the animal that has not gone elsewhere is crying out to be turned into salamis, thin or thick, spiced or not, hard or slightly soft to the squeeze.

Other animals provide material for charcuterie and cured goods. There are salamis and sausages made from beef and lamb. Of course there are. Some are worth being introduced to. Some are even worth eating, once or twice. But there is no doubt that, in the provision of these goods, the pig is king. Partly this has to do with our historical proximity to it. You need to be a farmer with serious land to raise cattle or sheep. 'But the pig is easy to raise,' says Bruce Aidells, renowned American sausage maker, and author of the *Complete Book of Pork*. 'And it doesn't require a lot of land.' Throughout the world, pigs have long been kept close to domestic settings – out back, or even underneath homes – as a waste-disposal unit with a pulse, and a kind of defence against food scarcity. In her 2003 study (published in the journal *Ethnos*) of the food politics of lardo di Colonnata, the cured back fat of the pig which is a speciality of Carrara in central Italy, Alison Leitch describes how in the eighteenth and nineteenth centuries most households would keep a pig. 'One of the by-products of these pigs, lardo or cured pork fat, thus constituted a kind of food safe for families in the region and was an essential daily source of calo-rific energy in the quarry worker's diet.'

In his classic mid-nineteenth-century book on pig husbandry – simply called *The Pig* – the English writer Samuel Sidney said, 'There is no savings bank for a labourer like a pig.' He wasn't wrong. Having been fed only on household waste, a sow could produce two litters of ten or more, twice a year. These would fatten very quickly and could then be sold off. The remaining animals would be kept and slaughtered in the winter, when the cold weather helped in the initial process of preservation. After that it was down to salt and spices, the processes which give us those glorious bacons, hams and salamis.

But proximity is not the only reason why the pig is favoured for charcuterie. Harold McGee, the American writer whose book *On Food and Cooking* is regarded as the key text for those interested in the science behind what happens with ingredients in our kitchens, attributes part of it to the flavour of the fat. Or, to be more precise, the lack of it. Both lamb and beef fat has a strong, distinct flavour. 'Pig fat has the advantage of being relatively neutral,' McGee writes. Bruce Aidells goes further. 'Pork fat also tends to be softer and creamier, whereas beef fat is really hard, which is not a great attribute when making ground meat products.' This, he says, may be down to the melting point. 'Plus there's the issue of the way the meat binds to itself when it's ground down for sausages or salamis. It's a natural process caused by the release of proteins which are soluble in salt solution. So by adding the salt as part of the curing process you create that bind. Pork simply binds better to itself than beef or lamb.' He also points out that when salted the muscle of beef or lamb can go very hard, 'whereas pork retains its succulence'.

So not only is the pig a walking, fully filled buffet table, it is biologically designed to be even more edible. There is only one problem with all this.

Pigs also happen to be smart.

Winston Churchill once commented that 'a pig can look a man in the eye and see his equal'. According to Donald Broom,

Emeritus Professor of Animal Welfare at Cambridge University, he was almost right. 'I think we would probably say that pigs are as complex in their behaviour and intellectual ability as children of maybe three years old,' he once told me. 'They respond to their surroundings in a complex way. We know now that a pig can understand what it sees in a mirror, and respond to that in the same way a person would do.'

Despite all the pejoratives attached to the animal's name – dirty pig, filthy pig – they are clean creatures, and will designate a latrine area and a clean living area given the opportunity to do so. They need stimulation, the opportunity to root around with their noses to investigate their surroundings, objects to play with, and the company of other pigs. Sadly they have not always been given it. Until twenty years ago or so the tethering of sows in the very late stages of pregnancy was commonplace in Britain, because it was believed that otherwise they would roll over and smother their own litters. Piglets, with little or no stimulation, in enclosed environments, would start biting each other's tails. The tethering of sows was outlawed in the UK two decades back, and was eventually outlawed across Europe, courtesy of a number of European Union directives issued between 2008 and 2013. However, the worst excesses of intensive pig farming are still practised in various places all over the world.

I asked Professor Broom whether he thought all this information about pigs presented the consumer with ethical dilemmas when it came to the question of eating them. He was clear that it did. 'When they know how sophisticated they are and how much they can suffer when kept in bad conditions, they would have the same view as me, which is that we should provide situations which result in very good welfare for the animals.'

The writer, editor and food campaigner Rosie Boycott knew exactly how the pork she ate had been raised because she was the one who had done the raising. In 2001 a high-flying career in newspapers hit the buffers when she departed the editorship of the *Daily Express*. Not long after that she was involved in a serious car crash. She retreated to her farm in Somerset and started buying pigs. 'The pigs were emotionally a huge salvation,' she says, looking back. 'I became absolutely devoted to and fascinated by them. They are so not what your sense of an animal is.' What started out as a few breeding pairs eventually became 140 animals living in fields and woods around the house. 'Pigs are smart,' she says. 'They sense when something is going on. And they love fires. We would sit around a bonfire – I would sometimes actually sit on the pigs – and they would love staring into the flames.'

And after all that, she would still take them to slaughter? No, not the original breeding animals, she says. She had given them names like the Earl and Empress of Dillington. She knew them. So not those. But the others? 'Yes, it was quite clear why we were keeping pigs. They're incredibly quickly stunned, then their throats are slit, bang, bang, bang. It's very quick.' She would help take them to the abattoir and once found herself outside with a few animals that, unstressed from the journey, fell asleep in the sunshine. 'I took a photograph of them. I thought, this is okay, they've had a good life.'

And did she eat the pork? 'Yes,' she says. 'And I felt okay about it.'

What about Professor Broom, one of the country's leading experts on animal welfare. Does he eat pork? 'Yes, I just make sure it has been raised in the right way.'

As Dr Annie Gray points out, the animals wouldn't exist in the first place if it wasn't for our desire to eat them. 'My view is that it is better to have lived a good life and died than to have lived no life at all. I'd rather eat a well-cared for, loved pig than eat no pork at all and abnegate responsibility for the way pigs are treated.'

There are going to be committed non-meat eaters who will

find this argument completely unconvincing and specious. Then again, no argument is likely to convince that group of people. There are first principles at play here. Either you believe animals are the equals of humans, in which case you are going to find eating their meat very tricky indeed, or you do not hold this view, and those tests do not apply.

I do not see animals as our equals. Like Annie Gray, I hold that what matters is the quality and manner of both their life and death. We each must take responsibility, within the constraints on our resources, for the manner in which the food we eat was produced. Pork is no different.

I am a pork-eating Jew. Which is to say that, while there is no God in my universe, I cannot deny my Jewishness, nor would I wish to. It is obvious in a certain noisiness and expansiveness, in a particular way of interacting with family and friends. I am rubbish at sports. I do not go on long country walks, and I will never own a boat. I could say it's about more than just getting the jokes in Woody Allen movies, but there is a lot of that too.

But these are all secular, cultural associations, and the dietary laws are religious. There have been a variety of theories as to where they came from (if we put aside the whole 'God told us to' business). Some historians have claimed it was a response to an understanding of pigs as literally unclean carriers of disease, though the evidence is sketchy. After all, it was long understood that pork could be a reservoir for infection and in particular trichinosis, a parasitic disease which can result in multiple unpleasant symptoms, but that didn't stop people eating it. They merely recognized that it had to be cooked properly. (Interestingly, very few of the recipes included in British cookbooks from the eighteenth and nineteenth centuries involving pig were for pork cooked from raw to be eaten immediately. They were almost all for preserved or cured items – a process which should have killed off parasites – like hams, salamis, pâtés and terrines.)

In another model the entire set of Judaic commandments was literally a code of law, designed to maintain both civic society and the cultural identity of the Jews as a discrete tribe, during the various periods of exile from Palestine, for example after the fall of the Second Temple in AD 70. In this model the Jews choose not to eat pork and refuse to mix milk with meat simply to emphasize that they are Jews. But this can work both ways. In her 1997 book, *The Singular Beast*, the French anthropologist Claudine Fabre-Vassas presents evidence from fourth-century theological literature that Christian communities didn't just become distinguished passively from the Jews because they carried on eating pork. They made an active choice to eat it, specifically to flag up the point. Weirdly, Fabre-Vassas identifies one Christian community in the Pyrenees which had a tradition of making a pork blood sausage to be eaten at Easter, which was known locally as 'The Jew'. But then we know there are precedents in language: there is, after all, the anti Semitic taunt of 'Jewish pig'. Which, all things considered, is bizarre.

Then again, pigs have always had a rough time when it comes to language. We may know pigs to be clever, but we talk about people being 'pig ignorant'. There's 'pig ugly'. Thoughtless, brutal men are 'selfish pigs' or, in the language of a few years ago, 'male chauvinist pigs'. And then there are the police, who have been called pigs at various times in the eighteenth, nineteenth and twentieth centuries.

The poor, maligned animal. It gives us so very much, and yet is so very traduced.

When I was a small child, we began every day at home with a cooked breakfast: bacon, sausages and eggs. Looking back, from the age of wholegrain and muesli, I find this odd especially as my mother had trained as a nurse and, by the time I turned up, was a well-respected health columnist. But times and advice changed. Within a few years we had moved to toast for breakfast, spread with something venerated for its polyunsaturated fats (when polyunsaturated fats were still venerated and we knew no better). Still, I recall the bacon I ate as a kid: the bronzed meat, the crisped fat, the hit of salt and savoury. On Saturday mornings when I was seven or eight I would slip down to the kitchen while my parents were still asleep, and make a cooked breakfast for myself and my older brother. For some reason I did this naked, a practice which only came to an end when I managed to pour boiling bacon fat over my hand and incur second-degree burns that required hospital treatment.

Happily I blamed myself, not the bacon. How could I blame bacon or any of those pork products that had given me so much? As far as I'm concerned, for me not to honour my pig would be illogical. And so I finish with a recipe which does just that. Yes, just the one, but it's a corker: a stew I have been making for years and which has never let me down. Plus, it's pig squared. The dear, sweet animal turns up in two forms.

Enjoy.

PORK, CHORIZO AND BUTTER BEAN STEW

I adore self-seasoning one-pot dishes, and this pork and chorizo stew is a perfect example. Get everything right at the beginning – and it's almost impossible to get it wrong – and it requires almost no care or attention thereafter. Usually a stew like this is served with some sort of carb – rice, say, or potatoes – but it's so dense and rich that it doesn't really need it. A hunk of warm crusty bread will usually suffice.

Serves 6

6 cooking chorizo sausages, piquancy to taste (3 spicy and 3 mild can save the stew from blowing your socks off, and make it child friendly)
olive oil
1 medium-sized onion, chopped
1.5kg pork for braising, cut into rough 3cm cubes
1 x 400g tin of chopped tomatoes
750ml chicken stock (from cube is fine)
1 x 400g tin of butter beans

- Heat the oven to 150°C/300°F/gas 2.
- Slice the chorizo into 1cm discs, putting a third of the slices to one side for later.
- Heat a little olive oil in a deep casserole pot with a lid, add the onion and sauté until soft.
- Add two-thirds of the chorizo and fry off so that it caramelizes and the orange, paprika-rich oil begins to run. Steal the occasional piece of chorizo, while muttering 'chef's prerogative' under your breath.
- When all the chorizo has been cooked, steal a couple more pieces, then add the pork in handfuls and brown it in the copper-coloured oil. It only needs to take on a little colour. As each batch is done, push it to the side

to make space for the next until it has all been cooked through and mixed in with the onion and the chorizo.

- Add the tomatoes and the stock and mix in until the meat is completely submerged by the liquor.
- Put the remaining discs of uncooked chorizo into the pot and stir in. Bring to a simmer. Strain the butter beans and add them too.
- Put on the lid, place in the oven, and don't look at it for 2 hours.
- To check whether the stew is ready, fish out a piece of pork. It should come apart easily when tugged at with a couple of forks. If it's not yet completely ready, just return to the oven for 20 minutes and check again. If the liquor is a little thin, put the casserole back on the hob without the lid, bring to a gentle boil and reduce the sauce. The stew can easily be prepared ahead of time, and quickly reheated when you need it. Arguably it's even better on day two, and it lends itself to being made in even larger volume.

A biblical prophet writes

I have a confession to make.

I am not your Moses, culinary or otherwise, and you are not my people. Each of us operates by a moral code and I do of course have mine. But the older I get the more suspicious I become of the doctrinaire; of those who operate in a sharp world of black and white, rather than the real world of smudge and uncertainty. There are any number of self-appointed food Taliban out there, determined to shower you with rules and instructions. Eat this, not that. Do that, not the other. And with the hard-nosed and doctrinaire tends to come a bloodlessness and puritanism which suck the very joy out of both life and dinner. What's more, a whole lot of it is utterly wrong, for being cast so starkly in black and white.

Even though I look great in the whole Moses outfit, believe me, I am not another one of those.

The age of the Internet has brought us many things: pictures of kittens in cardboard boxes; videos of truly appalling driving on Russian highways; a leaky valve for the once-unexpressed rage and fury which is a part of the human condition. But its main benefit is that it has given us all access to information. We no longer need to have expertise handed down from the mountain top, by middle-aged chaps pretending to be biblical prophets. We have at our fingertips the means by which to test every instruction that comes our way.

Which is what I implore you to do. I've given you my food commandments. Obviously I believe I have researched and argued each one brilliantly. I think you will eat so much better if you live by them. Certainly, if I ever see you eating a hot dog with a knife and fork or claiming that blueberries will protect you from cancer, I will despair, but mostly because I have failed to convince you. I will just have to keep my fingers crossed that I've done my job.

Meanwhile, it's your turn. Go make your own food commandments. Trust me. It's fun.

But do also make the pork and chorizo stew. You'll need something to sustain you through the hard work ahead. What's more, it's a belter. I promise.

In fact that really is a commandment. Get on with it.

Acknowledgements

I am hugely grateful to all those who gave their time to be interviewed for this book. They are named in the text. As well as doing so, my friend and fellow *Kitchen Cabinet* panellist Dr Annie Gray provided me with large numbers of academic papers. The brilliant doctorate student Anna Colquhoun did likewise. I would also like to thank: Helen Colley, for helping to pimp my granola and for other recipe advice; Sarah Cuddon, who produced *Jay Rayner Pigs Out*, the edition of *Archive on Four* I presented for BBC Radio 4, first broadcast on 26 December 2015, from which some of the interviews in Commandment 10 are taken; Jacob Kenedy, for his thoughts on the functionality of pigs for charcuterie; Michel Roux Jr, for giving my andouillette gratin recipe the once-over; Professor Paul Rozin, for providing vital links to his own work; Professor Alan Warde of Manchester University, for encouraging me to put the word 'sometimes' into the commandment to cook.

This is an entirely new piece of work, apart from a few passages in Commandment 6, the instruction to choose your dining companions very carefully, elements of which are taken from articles and columns first written for the *Observer Food Monthly*, namely: 'Eating alone' (31 January 2010); 'Slow eaters have lost their appetite for life' (13 November 2011); 'People who take ages to choose in restaurants just don't like food' (16 September 2012); 'A well-done steak isn't a food choice: it's a crime' (12 December 2010). I am grateful to Guardian Newspapers Limited for granting me permission to reproduce this writing and more generally for giving me a fabulous platform from which to get things off my chest.

My recent books and my live shows are intrinsically linked. I would therefore like to take this opportunity to thank Levon Biss for his work on both show and book marketing photography, Stela Gildea for her stage management on the photo shoot, Marcia Stanton for designing and making my Moses outfit (yes, there is one – come see the *Ten (Food) Commandments* show), Alex Fane and his assistant Jess Hughes at United Agents Music Management for tour booking and support, and for my superb colleagues in the Jay Rayner Quartet, Dave Lewis and Robert Rickenberg, who don't know it yet, but who will get to sit through the show countless times before they get to play.

Penguin Books has been a brilliant partner in this venture. Special thanks go to my editor, Joel Rickett, and to Poppy North, press person extraordinaire, who has also gone to extraordinary lengths to make sure books have been available for sale at each venue. Thank you, too, to my agent Jonny Geller of Curtis Brown for his continued wisdom and guidance.

As ever, my wife, Pat Gordon-Smith, read every page, added invaluable editorial advice and listened patiently as I blathered on excitedly about each new piece of research I had stumbled across. I couldn't have done it without her.

Finally, the idea for this book started with another publisher, who then made promises he couldn't keep. He asked that if I ever did publish the book elsewhere I would remember him. And so: hello, Iain.

February 2016, Brixton